TEILHARD REASSESSED

TEILHARD REASSESSED

A Symposium of Critical Studies in the
Thought of Père Teilhard de Chardin
attempting an Evaluation of his place
in contemporary Christian thinking

Edited by

ANTHONY HANSON

Professor of Theology,
The University of Hull

DARTON, LONGMAN & TODD

London

First published in Great Britain in 1970
by Darton, Longman & Todd Limited
85 Gloucester Road, London SW7
© 1970 Anthony Hanson
Printed in Great Britain at
the Pitman Press, Bath
ISBN 0 232 51108 X

Contents

v

89066

Introduction

This symposium originated in a series of lectures given in Truro under the auspices of the Department of Extra-Mural Studies of the University of Exeter. We acknowledge our indebtedness to Mrs Judith Shelton, Lecturer at the Cornwall Technical College, Camborne, and to Mrs Croose-Parry, of the Teilhard de Chardin Association, for their interest and energy in arranging these lectures and in encouraging us to go ahead with the publication of a symposium, I would myself wish to thank Canon Harold Blair for beginning the task of organising the symposium and for his willing collaboration in the same task when it was later handed on to me.

It is not easy today to make a cool assessment of Pierre Teilhard de Chardin. This is partly because he is a figure about whom it is difficult to be neutral. He seems to invite either hostility or partisanship, and there has been no lack of these phenomena ever since the publication of his philosophical works began. Another reason that makes assessment difficult is that, like Gerard Manley Hopkins, he published (or was permitted to publish) so little in his lifetime. This means that he did not have the benefit of his contemporaries' criticism, and was therefore bound to be a bit of a Narcissus. As in the case of Dietrich Bonhoeffer, we do not always know what he meant. Thirdly, he touches so many aspects of thought that he is very vulnerable to the attack of the specialist. But such thinkers are badly needed in a time when everyone is complaining of the fragmentation of knowledge. We must often be prepared to give him credit for what he tried to do even when we criticise the way he did it.

At the same time a reassessment by a number of students of his work from England is perhaps timely just now. Teilhard's influence in this country shows no sign of decreasing. Those who offer to lecture on his work up and down the country report a sustained interest in him among a very wide section of the public, by no means confined to what would normally be called the religious public. He acts apparently as something of a cross-bench figure: he seems to have something to say to both Catholic and Protestant—and to the Humanist also perhaps. He certainly makes a special appeal to some scientists. It is also worth mentioning that Teilhard may represent an intellectual link between these islands and the Continent. This is particularly welcome in view of the fact that in philosophy one school has established a virtual monopoly in English universities, and that it has a tendency dogmatically to ignore the study of other schools more popular on the Continent.

Dr Turk begins our Symposium with an essay that estimates Teilhard's significance as a philosopher of evolution. Next comes Dr Dyson's explanation of Teilhard's dialectic. The Revd R. B. Smith follows with two essays dealing with the place of evil and the meaning of creation in Teilhard's thought. Canon Blair then examines the idea of progress, so important in Teilhard's scheme of things; and adds a brief essay on some aspects of his doctrine of incarnation. Then comes the Revd W. J. P. Boyd's interesting comparison of Teilhard with some leading figures in modern Protestant theology. Last of all comes my own attempt to assign Teilhard a place in the category of prophet, on the basis of what he has to say to the Church about doctrine.

This is not a piece of group thinking, but a symposium, and each contributor is alone responsible for his opinions.

Anthony Hanson

University of Hull

ONE

The Idea of Biological and Social Progress in the System of Teilhard de Chardin

F. A. TURK

'The cunning writer will choose an indefinable subject; for he can then set down his theory of what it is; and next, at length, his conception of what it is not – and lo! his paper is covered.' O. Henry (William Sidney Porter 1862–1910), *The Country of Elusion*.

Introduction

O. Henry's sly, sardonic shaft can all too easily find its mark in any writer on the philosophy of Teilhard de Chardin; indeed, it seems to me that most have already been picked off in this manner. If I state my belief here that much of the now celebrated book by Nicolas Corte on Teilhard[1] is in

---

[1] Corte, N., *Pierre Teilhard de Chardin: His Life and Spirit* (London, 1960). As example of the kind of muddled writing into which the earnestness of the author leads him, here he is on 'his theory of what it is', p. 58: After quoting Teilhard at the beginning of *The Phenomenon of Man* in the passage in which he says 'the book I am offering here (is) to be read . . . only and exclusively as a scientific memoir', Corte continues 'So that is clear. It is a scientist speaking to his peers. He speaks the language they know and love.' This may be very strongly doubted but what is certain is that if we accept Popper's definition of a scientific statement as one capable of disproof then possibly not more than one eighth of the book's statements are, in this sense, scientific. The rest of the same embarrassing paragraph of Corte's had perhaps best be kindly

like manner such a casualty, it is not, in any sense, with the intention of being needlessly controversial but simply to point out, very succinctly, a hazard which faces all of us. Where so many and so famous have failed it is with obvious temerity that one essays to do better.

The reasons for this failure appear to me not really far to seek. They are (1) Teilhard's curiously visionary metaphysic resting on an epistemology of the utmost indefiniteness. Teilhard seems to have some extremely interesting epistemological implications in his system of which we catch glimpses from time to time. So he says: 'To make room for thought in the world, I have needed to "interiorise" matter.' If one were to attempt to throw light on this by the comparative method essayed in this article one might possibly with some profit compare the implications of Teilhard's views with those of Cassirer (*The Philosophy of Symbolic Forms*) (1923–1929). Here is the whole difference between the neo-realist and the neo-idealist, the latter position showing fewer difficulties. (2) A method riddled with inconsistencies and quite elementary logical errors. (3) A terminology often obscure and difficult and one in which the meanings of the terms shift disconcertingly. (4) An almost complete lack of documentation or comparison in the work as a whole. This is very characteristic of him. The references which he appends even to his scientific papers could hardly be considered other than scanty, judged by contemporary standards. It is difficult to judge the real extent of his reading especially his philosophical reading and this notwithstanding the lists given in Cuénot's *Teilhard de Chardin*. It is true that

---

left for those who understand it. Again (p. xiii) Corte says 'He (i.e. Teilhard) is not concerned to "reconcile" evolution with anything'. Yet Teilhard himself is saying in a letter dated 4 December 1951 (*Letters from a Traveller*, p. 264) that one level of his activity is 'To pursue my effort to re-think Christology and Christianity in terms of a humanity in process of biological convergence'. This looks like reconciliation indeed! It must be stressed once more that my purpose here is not to ridicule Corte's book but merely to show the relevance of O. Henry's dictum.

we have certain hearsay evidence from friends that his studies over the widest field of learning were profound, cf. the account quoted by Cuénot which tells of Teilhard's deep knowledge of parapsychology, analytical psychology and related fields. This might, of course, be an accurate report but it is difficult to evaluate. The matter is not made easier by reason of the somewhat enthusiastic habit of most of his French apologists of giving us long lists of the distinguished scholars in many fields that he visited and impressed.[1] This hint of almost vulgar intellectual snobbery is not, of course, uncommon in the writings of advocates of many different systems who wish to impress an audience with their scientific respectability. The *argumentum ad verecundiam* has always had a curious subsidiary role in systems of Christian apologetics based on the conclusions of 'current' science; one has but to think of the popularity of Sir James Jeans in this respect, in the 'fringe' theological writings of the late 1920s and 1930s. (5) His almost total lack of acknowledgment to any previous philosophers, even those who seem to form the obvious source of much of his theory, e.g. General Smuts, with whom Teilhard was acquainted and whose *Holism and Evolution* we should have expected him to have read.

Nevertheless, in fairness to Teilhard, he appears to have seen, and to go some way to acknowledging, these matters. On page 290 of *The Phenomenon* he says: 'Among those who have attempted to read this book to the end, many will close it, dissatisfied and thoughtful, wondering whether I have been leading them through facts, through metaphysics or through dreams . . . My one hope is that I have made the reader feel both the reality, difficulty and urgency of the problem and, at the same time, the scale and the form which the solution must take.'

Most controversy about the Teilhardian system stems I suppose, ultimately, from that word 'must' in the last sentence. It is the inevitability of Teilhard's kind of solution

[1] A very friendly exposition of some of these – mostly discounted – will be found, for example, in Prof. I. Barbour's 'Five Ways of Reading Teilhard', *The Teilhard Review*, Vol. 3, No. 1 (1968), pp. 3–20.

that is in dispute. That he himself did not care very much
what heading his theory and methods were classified under is
obvious enough from the above quotation, but that itself will
only sharpen our dilemma when we come to attempt any
appraisal of his work.

How then shall we ourselves – given some vague feeling of
consent to the proposition that Teilhard's intuitions may be
of value to us – deal with this extraordinary system which is
demonstrably not scientific, is philosophically *'jejune'* and
logically faulty? That some scientific 'fact' enters into it is
undeniable. That it is in some sense a philosophy has been
admitted by most of his readers, and yet the more sophisticated or less committed will surely be uncomfortably aware
that it is perilously near those metaphysical systems which, I
believe, the great Kant said were to be likened to a man
holding a sieve and another attempting to milk a billy goat
into it!

But if it is not a philosophy; if neither the method nor the
conclusions may, in any strict sense, be accounted scientific,
what, in fact, is it? Has it value? If so, how best may we use
it?[1] Firstly, we must be quite clear that, because a writing
is not scientific (in any closely definable sense) it is not

[1] It is obvious that a work like Teilhard's *Phenomenon* differs in many
respects from the mystico-theological writings of some other notable
scientists, e.g. Sir Isaac Newton's *Lexicon Propheticum* (London, 1737) with
its odd superstructure based on the nature of the sacred cubit of the
Jews, yet that it has some, though distant, relationship to that curious
category is hardly to be doubted. But again, there are to be seen affinities,
of a kind, with such antithetical writers as William Blake. Blake was
nothing if not practical even about his visions; indeed, he recommends
his friends to 'work up imagination to the state of vision' and, even if
reasoning and nature switched Blake 'off' and Teilhard 'on' – if one may
so express it – yet *The Book of Urizen* (1794) has at least similarities of
method with Teilhard's *Le Milieu Divin*. As Blake saw the necessity for
working at the achievement of vision so does Teilhard recommend a not
dissimilar approach in his chapter 'Detachment through Action' to the
end that the Christian may encounter God 'in the entire field of his
actions in the perceptible world'. Both certainly saw 'the marvellous
mounting force contained in things' (*Le Milieu Divin*, pp. 44–47). In
this matter too I feel that the approach to Teilhard's 'philosophy' by a
comparative method may yield us certain insights of value.

therefore valueless – even to science. Indeed it is now, I believe, generally admitted that science in the past has come on as many of its findings by 'playing hunches' as it has by generating them from accepted and tested fact. At the very least, whatever may give a new direction to our scientific insights or intuitions is surely not valueless. That Teilhard was always more at home 'playing his hunches' is what we might have expected from such a mind. An example of this is his theory of 'continentalisation' and his changing attitude to Wegener's theory of Continental Drift (Cuénot pp. 339–340). That he finally abandoned Wegener's theory within a few years of the turn of the tide of geological thought and of the findings that appear now to vindicate it, is a sad quirk of the fate that dogged several of his scientific theories. Even in Africa, the continent that appears to have played the larger part in Teilhard's continentalisation theories, recent studies show the drift still continues and that at least two parts of the East African rift system are still mobile (see Drs Gass, I. G. and Gibson, I. L., *Nature* (1969) 221, p. 926 and 221, p. 1018). The example is a very typical one even to the terminology and might provide anyone interested in the problems of 'style' in science with useful data. It was perhaps enough for Teilhard that someone's theory – some set of facts accumulated by others or yet some experience of his own – should generate a larger, 'nobler' more 'mystically' significant vision. Although I am aware that many eminent scientists think otherwise (pre-eminently Professor Medawar) I must confess that I see nothing intrinsically detrimental in this, providing (a) that it will generate other interpretations that are more productive, more verifiable, more rigorous or more definitive, and (b) that one is ready to discard the theory when closer reasoning increases the number of its inconsistencies sufficiently to make it untenable. Many of those who, not to arouse our suspicions, seem to me to protest too much the 'scientific' nature of Teilhard's work, appear to overlook this fact or, at least, to accord it only minor importance. If we discard Teilhard's system because it is not 'scientific' or even because it is often grossly illogical in its exposition, we shall, in my view, be guilty of maximum error. It differs from Newton's apocalyptic writings and Blake's visionary ones precisely because it is more relevant to our own climate of knowledge than the first and is potentially more generative of further 'gestalts' than the second.

Although no logician, I strongly suspect that this could, without too much trouble, be shown to lead to a series of statements that were, in essence, a sequence of tautologies. For an important insight into this as to the unfalsifiable nature of certain kinds of statements one should see Munz, P., *Relationship and Solitude* (London 1964), where the following important statement is made on page 81. '. . . the only evidence we have about the World is tautology. And since tautology is compatible with any proposition other than a self-contradictory one, we know nothing of the World that would not be compatible with any metaphysical theory. The same is true, of course, for scientific theories about the symbol picture.' And again, on page 48 'We must conclude, therefore, that the only thing that can be said about the World is a tautology such as "the World worlds" ''. A careful study of Professor Munz's important work provides some valuable material for the evaluation of Teilhard's theory and demonstrates the extra difficulties and limitations it suffers in having such an elaborate superstructure raised on such tenuous epistemological foundations.

It is an advantage of such an elementary comparative system of study as I have tried to practise in this essay that it avoids consideration, for the time at least, of these epistemological difficulties and deficiencies. It examines, or better, throws an oblique light across Teilhard's system by considering it singly in relation to others that have been founded upon, roughly, the same range of data. In short, if we read Teilhard's account of evolution in isolation, then his facts are 'coloured' by his theory, both as to selection, interpretation and presentation. If, however, we look at Teilhard's evolutionary theory in relation to, and in the context of, other theories, we should, it seems, eventually be able to make adjustments and modifications which will provide us with an 'objective', if only very partial, 'apparatus criticus' of Teilhard's whole system. I am aware that this is but a first and very elementary step and that its relevance is strictly limited but it has I believe a significance which will emerge further at the end of this essay.

These are some – not all – of the values that I myself see in Teilhard's philosophy, but how indeed can we best use it to produce such new scientific 'gestalts'?

The complete answer to this, as I see it, lies beyond the scope of this essay and it must await exposition for a further occasion, but there is I believe something of smaller scope that may be usefully undertaken in this connection: indeed, something that must be undertaken.

In method Teilhard's system is, of course, a phenomeno-logical one although in a wider sense perhaps than writers like Husserl have conceived of phenomenology. It is of a type that Prof. Laird called 'ostensive analysis' in so far as it makes an attempt to find patterns in nature, the contempla-tion of which will yield general truths. But with such a system it is, of course, important to know both how the facts are selected and that they tell the *whole* truth. There is indeed an additional hazard; it is that the system that eventuates will itself colour, contort or confuse these 'facts'. Since any of the readers of such works as Teilhard de Chardin's will have, at best, a competence or expertise in but a limited field – however extensive it may seem to those whose attainments lie in other spheres – it may help us to a more just appraisal if we view his reading of nature alongside that of other workers interested in the same facts as he was. Because almost all his philosophical writing is so poorly documented that the inexpert reader's task is the harder, then this essay is essentially such an attempt to make it just a little lighter.

In short, this is to expound (and expand) the system, not in its own terms but *comparatively*; to provide, that is, part of the background of other views on selected Teilhardian themes which is exactly what we find wanting when we read works like *The Phenomenon of Man*, *La Vision du Passé*, or *The*

Future of Man. It is as an example of what I envisage necessary in this respect, that this essay is designed to look over, very briefly, the central theme of 'Progress' in his Philosophy.

The Idea of Progress essential to both Teilhard and his system

In reading his biographers, and more so in reading Teilhard's letters, I have come to the inescapable conclusion that he had a deep emotional need to be assured of the reality of progress. Early in life there had come to him (1909–1912) 'consciousness of the radical drift, ontological and total, of the universal'. As Cuénot (*loc. cit.* page 35) says, his view of the cosmos was essentially convergent[1] and, I suppose therefore, in a sense, essentially teleological. Whether this was much more than a feeling of conviction arising from his spiritual needs and theological conditioning or whether it arose from a palaeontologist's opinion of the necessity of convergence and even orthogenesis, I find difficult to determine. The difficulty is made no easier by an obscurity in Cuénot's writing in this same passage: he says 'Teilhard although vitalist – or, more exactly, a supporter of orthogenesis – did allow mechanisms their part (their very great part, particularly in elementary forms of life) but he credited them with only a minor role in complex forms of life. . . .' I entirely fail to understand a necessary connection such as Cuénot seems to see between vitalism and orthogenesis.

[1] This is certainly so: but I believe non-scientific readers of Teilhard will hardly be aware how much evidence there is for a divergent, ever differentiating interpretation of evolution. As one example, it now seems that all forms of life, from bacteria to man, use the same genetic code and almost the same chemistry in the cell to translate it. What appears to be proof of this is the recent work of Laycock, D. S. and Hunt, J. A. (*Nature*, March, 1969, No. 221, p. 1118) showing that a bacterium inhabiting the human intestine will synthesise the protein of rabbit's blood when subjected to the 'genetic instructions' of the rabbit. It is true that Teilhard saw something of this 'common mechanism' (*Phenomenon*, page 95) and yet, as it were, read the series the 'wrong' way. This is not to show Teilhard's 'convergent' picture as wrong or without value but to suggest that it does give grounds for supposing that it arose in his own deeper spiritual needs and desires.

But there are other difficulties in the obscurities of Teilhard's own style and the exuberance of thought which forces it on under the compulsion of an almost manic excitement. Consider this passage from his 1943 paper.[1] 'There below, as early Man, only little – here above, a modern Man very much "cerebralised" and "socialised". What does this difference mean? Obviously, only one interpretation can be given of the curve. What the prehistorians have so patiently registered point after point, during the last fifty years, is nothing less than the trace left by Humanity moving persistently towards a higher individual and collective consciousness.' It may be; *but* 'only one interpretation'? Then comes a footnote on the terms 'cerebralised' and 'socialised': in this he says 'Both terms expressing the same process, since, in Man, socialisation is nothing but an association of brains'. And on the following page, 'As far as "cerebralisation" is concerned, of course, it is possible that the human brain has reached by now the maximum of complexity and we cannot proceed any further, but in the direction of socialisation we have scarcely begun to advance. In this matter, therefore, our physical and spiritual future is almost unlimited and it lies largely in our heads and hands.'

That there is intellectual muddle in the confusion between 'cerebralisation' and 'socialisation' in this somewhat breathlessly ecstatic passage will be apparent to most readers with some biological knowledge. Social life appears in some ways to depend upon only certain areas and functions of the cerebral hemispheres, e.g. the 'damping down' of the impulses from the brain stem. Quite as much depends on the brain itself and indeed one would suppose that the brain stem must be, at least, involved in the basic psychic mechanisms of group life, i.e. sympathy, suggestion and imitation. Again the function of some areas of the cerebral hemispheres might be thought to act as much against socialisation as for it, e.g. those that project the individual's field of action into the future. Yet granted this muddle, one cannot but feel that

[1] Teilhard de Chardin, *Fossil Men: Recent Discoveries and Present Problems* (Peking, 1943).

such sentences express a deeply felt and sincerely held emotional need for the general idea of progress – for in fact 'the something more, the somewhere to be going'. Progress – the belief in progress – was an essential part of Teilhard's troubled spirit: it was this that did most to reconcile in later life his scientific knowledge with his spiritual yearnings, his guilt feelings about his urge to speculation and his irrepressible need to feel that he comprehended what the otherwise to him incomprehensible Christian God was about.

As one of several pieces of supporting evidence we need only cite a passage in a letter on the 9th May, 1940 to his cousin in which he says 'Are not such moments (i.e. of suffering) necessary to accustom us to that gesture, essential not only in death but in life, which consists in allowing ourselves to rest upon Him who sustains and upholds us right outside all the tangible things to which we feel so strong an instinct to cling? It is undoubtedly by being accustomed in this way that we shall finally be released from speculation.' But this Islamic surrender to the will of God was not for him – or not for long; his could never be the mysticism of the *via negativa*. Less than a year later (12 January, 1941) he is writing 'Everything can be forced and led out by a group of men united by a common faith in the spiritual future of the earth. We must take up again on a sounder scientific basis and as a more exact philosophical concept the idea (or if you prefer it the 'myth') of progress. This is essentially the setting in which I see the simultaneous rebirth of humanism and Christianity.' Yet, by the time *The Phenomenon of Man* appears that prudent phrase about the 'myth' of progress has disappeared. On page 230 of the English edition we find him saying 'If progress is a myth, that is to say, if faced by the work involved we can say: "what's the good of it all", our efforts will flag. With that the whole of evolution will come to a halt – because we are evolution.' He himself had to hope before he could summon energy for any activity – a sure indication of the incipient neurosis with which he made such valiant and successful attempts to come to terms, for, as he says in a footnote to page 233 of *The Phenomenon*:

'All conscious energy is, like love, founded on hope.' That others should labour for the solace of the work, from pleasurable interest of activity, even simply for the fulfilment of their own nature, was apparently an experience he neither shared nor understood.

To me, it seems clear enough that Teilhard had a great and ever erupting need to convince himself that progress was real and that it could, in a sense, be controlled by Man. This was essential to his system and his system was essential to reconcile this spiritual need with what he conceived to be the truths of science and it had to act as a catalyst upon all the conflicting elements that tormented him for sixty years albeit apparently hidden from his friends and close associates. Finally, in another letter to his cousin he says, 'I feel at the age of sixty I have at last found or pinned down my true vocation. Now the question is to find the right platform, the right significant act.' By 1940 he had clearly seen the need to examine 'progress'. By 1941, he seems to have accepted the actuality of it without much further examination, so far as the evidence is known to me. Progress then is an essential element, perhaps *the* essential element, in his philosophy and yet, by a strange and possibly revealing quirk of circumstance, I do not think that you will find this word as an item in the index of any one of his major works.

There has always been some difficulty for biologists in defining, from the evidence, wherein biological progress resides; by what precise criteria we shall recognise it in the pattern of evolutionary sequence. The old-fashioned evolutionary trees of animals and plants are, as everyone knows, always shown upright! This arrangement seems to make clear that evolution progresses from 'lower' to 'higher'. Yet, to the biologist, the 'lower' are as perfectly adapted to their special habitats as the 'higher' – sometimes, maybe, better and more perfectly so. The so-called 'higher' level may be marked by increased complexity, improved rationalisation or greater versatility in reacting to environmental stimuli, but, in a changing environment, it can often have upon it the shadow of its future extinction. Since Teilhard himself was primarily a stratigrapher and secondarily a palaeontologist, we will glance first at the theme of biological progress.

Biological Progress

The view of life sketched in the last paragraph is a very ancient one. Certainly it is as old as Anaximander of Miletus (*c.* 611–*c.* 546 B.C.), who says, 'Living creatures arose from the moist element as it was evaporated by the sun. . . . The first animals were produced in moisture, each enclosed in a prickly bark. As they advanced in age they came out upon the drier part and when the bark broke off they survived for a short time. . . . Human beings are like other animals, namely fish, in the beginning. . . . At first human beings arose in the inside of fishes and, after having been reared like sharks (i.e. the live bearing ones such as the Mako shark) and become capable of protecting themselves, they were finally cast ashore and took to land.' Here surely is the beginning of the vision of the evolutionary pattern of nature the realisation of which was to be perhaps the chief ingredient in the making of the modern world. In the last forty years no reputable scientist has failed to see in nature the dominant thematic pattern of evolution.

But must evolution simply progress or is it merely change? Is it essentially a quality of life, a condition of its existence like respiration, or is it in some sense an 'overplus', arguing a purpose – however remote and mysterious or however capable of blinding revelation – lying behind all natural phenomena? Teilhard would, I believe, have seen the purpose very clearly. On page 294 of *The Phenomenon* he describes God as the 'Centre of centres' and says 'and so exactly, so perfectly, does this coincide with omega point that doubtless I should never have ventured to envisage the latter or formulate the hypothesis rationally if, in my consciousness as a believer, I had found not only its speculative model but also its living reality'. The purpose of evolution was therefore, for Teilhard, the realisation of a personal God. How extraordinarily revealing that passage is! Whether this realisation of the omega point was in any way similar to

Anaximander's view that all things must return to their origin does not seem to me determinable, for I have looked in vain through much of Teilhard's work for a definitive statement on this. In one way or another he appears to go no further than 'A God who brings to birth, in the heart of things, the successive stages of His work' (*The Vision of The Past*, Chapter 5, note 1). It is difficult, it is true, to find any similarity between this and Anaximander's overriding principle of justice and reparation, although they were considering essentially the same set of facts.

However this may be, it is certain that Teilhard's views agree very closely with those of most other biologists when he speaks of the origin of life except that he passionately argues for a single origin. 'We must postulate', he says 'at this particular moment of terrestrial evolution (i.e. the origin of life) a coming to maturity, a threshold, a crisis of the first magnitude, the beginning of a new order.'[1] Additionally, he says that this 'awakening or jump (i) *could*, or better (ii) *was bound* to happen'. This seems to me of the utmost importance not merely for Teilhard's own system but because it yields to us a pattern fraught with as much significance as evolution itself.[2] On this view – and I hold it to be the correct one – there is, at the heart of existence a pre-determinism. Indeed such a pre-determinism seems to run through the whole of Teilhard's exposition even although he clearly envisages, at least for Man, a very large element of free will.

Yet this may be indeed a pattern in Evolution also seen –

[1] *The Phenomenon of Man*, page 79.

[2] The idea is not, of course, new. H. J. Muller in 1921 ('Mutation', a paper read before the Int. Eng. Cong. N. York and published in 1923 in *Eugenics, Genetics and the Family*, Vol. 1, pp. 106–112) called attention to the fact that given any mutating system capable of the replication of its forms, then life and evolution would automatically follow. Forty-five years later that author passed on from this to the strict definition of an organism as that which possesses the potentiality of evolving by Natural Selection. All that has happened since in molecular biology has gone to support that view. The functional purposiveness of the bacteriophage is in the structure of its nucleic acid and its informational function, i.e. at the molecular level.

although possibly not very clearly – by Teilhard. Freedom increases as Life evolves,[1] and inevitably so. The increase of this freedom in a nexus of pre-determined events, may indeed be more important, more basic, than the evolution of consciousness itself, an event that is perhaps no more than the final expression to date of that same ineluctable drift to freedom. I am, of course, ignoring here the further problem that both complete determinism and freedom are categories generated by the symbols invented by or emerging from the *Gemütszustanden* of the evolved consciousness. This line of thought, obviously outside the scope of the present essay, is yet very worth while further consideration. If progress means directional movement as, for example, from lower to higher or simpler to complex, then indeed this is progress and Teilhard was on firm enough ground in invoking it as a pattern inherent in the evolution of life. But if by progress we mean movement towards a goal and, by implication, the fulfilment of either purpose or promise, we shall have to look both harder and further, for this second kind of progress (one which is, of course, the whole *raison d'être* of Teilhard's system) is not easily to be derived, in any illative sense, from the first.

To speak of 'lower' and 'higher' of course, in this connection, begs the question to a large extent. For nearly two hundred years scientists and philosophers have concerned themselves not a little with the search for really significant distinguishing characters by means of which we might operate such a grading. Erasmus, Darwin, Lamarck, Goethe and Cuvier – the last of whom showed that the more primitive forms are earlier in time – all made contributions to the problem at the end of the eighteenth and the beginning of the nineteenth centuries. It was indeed Goethe himself who laid down the principle that biological progress consisted of increasing differentiation and centralisation of structure.

[1] The late Prof. C. A. F. Pantin (*The Relations between the Sciences* Cambridge University Press, 1968) defines one of the four chief differences differentiating the living and the non-living as the fact that organisms *do* things whereas things *happen* to inanimate matter.

Goethe, in fact, published this interpretation in its entirety in 1817: *Zur Naturwissenschaft überhaupt, besonders zur Morphologie* (Stuttgart and Tübingen), but he seems to have had the germ of the idea in the *Erster Entwurf einer allgemeinen Einleitung in die vergleichende Anatomie* of 1795. It appears in his writings under the guise of the law of progression marked by increasing 'dissimilarity' and 'subordination' of parts. This view is not without a certain relevance to Teilhard's theories, in which there is to be discerned his marked emotional distress in contemplating such a dichotomy in the evolutionary process. We can see it in the passages on page 263 of *The Phenomenon*, e.g. 'in trying to separate itself as much as possible from others, the element individualises itself; but in doing so it becomes retrograde and seeks to drag the world backwards towards plurality and into matter'. Goethe's acceptance of the paradox of differentiation and centralisation seems less distraught and more in agreement with both the evidence and present knowledge: to some it will possibly appear both nobler and humbler. Many years ago Sir Julian Huxley considered this matter of differentia- tion (*The Individual in the Animal Kingdom*, Cambridge, 1912) and the significance of the resulting individuality with this conclusion: '. . . there are many grades, many degrees, and many kinds of individuality, and each individual must be judged on its merits, as something really new.' Not many biologists would wish to quarrel with that today, I imagine, except possibly to point out the value of individuals that stabilise the type, for too rapid a differentiation has often (but not always) led to too certain an extinction. The relevance of this problem to social progress I shall return to later in this essay.

By the mid-nineteenth century these two principles of anagenesis or progressive evolution were being emphasised by writer after writer and, under the influence of the great Milne-Edwards[1] they became the pre-occupation of the zoological writings of the time.[2] Some authors, like Prof.

[1] Milne-Edwards, H., *Introduction à la zoologie générale* (Paris, 1851).
[2] For a discussion of the history of these and cognate ideas see: Franz,

Bronn,[1] added certain other patterns which they considered could be observed in nature. Thus Bronn himself called attention to the seeming universality of the principle of the Division of Labour and – less universal but almost equally interesting – the decrease in the number of the single parts of organisms and their tendency to show a progressive shifting of external organs to the interior. We do not know whether or not Teilhard attached any significance to these features in the terms of his theory.

In the 1920s and 30s Franz and Plate gave much attention to the characteristics of biological perfection. The former author (Franz, 1935)[2] accepts only the criteria of survival-value and, paradoxically enough, by inference, stabilisation! Plate[3] considered that 'Biological perfection arises from an harmonious increase of the number, complexity and efficiency of adaptations'. More original perhaps, and at this point in history more illuminating, was the contribution of Sewertzoff,[4] who thought that 'progress is shown by the acquisition of new characters that increase the energy of the vital processes of the organism'. This he proposed calling 'aromorphosis' and exemplified it by a study of the evolution of the vertebrate lower jaw. Aromorphosis is an aspect of

V., *Die Vervollkommung in der lebenden Natur. Eine Studie über ein Naturgesetz* (Jena, 1920); Franz, V., *Geschichte der Organismen* (Jena, 1924), and Uschmann, G., *Der morphobiologische Vervollkommungsbegriff bei Goethe und seinep roblemgeschichtlichen Zusammenhänge* (Jena, 1939) – the last especially of interest.

[1] Bronn, H. G., *Allgemeine Einleitung in die Naturgeschichte* (Stuttgart, 1853).

[2] Franz, V., *Der biologische Fortschritt. Die Theorie der Organismen – geschichtlichen Vervollkommung* (Jena, 1935). In this he says 'The degree of perfection in a type of organism (species, genus, order and so on) will depend upon the efficiency of the mechanisms serving to maintain the existence of the type.' (Quoted in Rensch, B., *Evolution above the Species Level*, New York, 1959.)

[3] Plate, L. *Die Abstammungslehre* (Jena, 1925) and 'Über Vervollkommung Anpassung und die Unterscheidung von niederen und höheren Tieren', *Zool. Jahber. Abt. allgem. Zool*, vol. 45, pp. 745–798 (1928).

[4] Sewertzoff, A. N., *Morphologische Gesetzmässigkeiten der Evolution* (Jena, 1931).

biological progress that might well have appealed to Teilhard (*The Phenomenon of Man*, p. 28) who appears to have thought that 'the energies of life seem unable to spread in one region or take on a new form except at the expense of a lowering elsewhere'. This was not a new idea,[1] but it seems nevertheless a very true one, and moreover one which had considerable repercussions when applied to the social evolution of Man. Teilhard might well have pointed, for example, to the aromorphic[2] character of the neolithic revolution – of which he wrote at length – but doubtless, as he himself would have seen, this was not to be achieved without a corresponding decline in other aspects of human life. Both of these principles appear to be demonstrable as patterns of organic evolution.

In terms of any exact expression of his views on the subject, Teilhard seems relatively uncommitted to any theory of what brings about this procession of 'progressive' forms. Authors like von Nägeli, Gaudry and Korschinsky,[3] in the two decades following the year 1880, certainly thought that it came about by reason of something truly innate – a kind of drive to perfection – and Gaudry at least did not hesitate to call this an activity of the divine. Although in some respects Teilhard's views are in something of the same category as those three writers,[4] yet in other, and more important respects, they certainly differ. Writing all of half a century later, Teilhard was bound to accept far more of the Darwinian standpoint than they had felt it necessary to do. Yet he, like them, has recourse to some inner principle 'which alone', he says, 'could explain its irreversible advance towards higher psychisms'.

[1] Demoor, J., Massart, J. and Vandervelde, E., *Evolution by Atrophy in Biology and Sociology* (London, 1899).

[2] Aromorphosis refers to that form of new character which is marked as one showing progressive morphological and physiological evolution.

[3] von Nägeli, C., *Mechanisch-physiologische Theorie der Abstammungslehre* (Munich and Leipzig, 1884). Gaudry, A., *Essai de paléontologie philosophique* (Paris, 1896) and Korschinsky, S., 'Heterogenesis und Evolution', *Naturwiss. Wochenschr.*, vol. 14, pp. 273–278 (1899).

[4] Teilhard many times put emphasis on what he designated 'The Impetus of Life'.

Perhaps the struggle which is being waged today in the field of biology over the theory of orthogenesis prevents a cool appraisal of Teilhard's beliefs in this respect. If, as I believe, in full agreement with Teilhard, orthogenesis should eventually prove to be a demonstrable pattern in the web of life, then I think his view of some 'within' (to use his own term) will have to rank for serious consideration. At this point in history the *furore* created by the exciting work on desoxyribonucleic acid and related matters in molecular biology has given to such aspects of evolution a kind of fustian fatuity for the new generation of workers. This is an accident of history – a veering of scientific taste and style; eventually it will pass quietly into the accepted corpus of scientific fact and the minds of yet a further generation of biologists will be free once again to examine with more tolerant appraisal some of these 'fringe' views of ancient pedigree. In this respect Teilhard's may prove to wear better than many orthodox zoologists would now suppose.

In this connection, I have come to think of the footnote on page 149 of *The Phenomenon of Man* as one of the most important contributions which that book makes to scientific thought. A few years ago the late Prof. Graham Cannon published a book which, in essence, was a defence of the neo-Lamarckian theory and an attack on the presently established orthodoxy of neo-Darwinism. (Cannon, H. G., *The Evolution of Living Things*, Manchester, 1958.) Two themes of prime importance were woven into the author's exposition of his views in this book: firstly, a challenge to the doctrine that the blind chance of natural selection accounted by itself for the production of new organs and organisms; secondly, that the gene theory cannot explain the capacity of the organism to admit new characters; that, in fact, the organism so adjusts the functioning of its existing parts in the process of reacting to the results of mutation or re-combination that it virtually constitutes a new organism. It is difficult to understand either the extremely unfavourable reviews the book had in some quarters when it first appeared or the almost total lack of attention it has received since it appeared. Professor Cannon sets out the grounds of his attack on the neo-Darwinist extremely lucidly on page 115 and everyone interested in attempting to discover the true basis and significance of Teilhard's views should give this page careful reading and unbiased reflection.

More deeply involved in Teilhard's view of Life and its mechanisms is the restatement made by Cannon of the four laws of Lamarckism and his demonstration that the 4th law – and the only one associated in the popular, and even 'expert' mind, with his name – is redundant. The author clearly demonstrates that the central position of the Lamarckian hypothesis is occupied by the 2nd law. This states 'the production of a new organ in an animal body results from a new need which continues to make itself felt and from a new movement that this need brings about and maintains.' Later in the book, Cannon has this to say (p. 137): 'The neo-Mendelian attributes all these amazing adaptations merely to a fantastic succession of lucky hits. Lamarck says that they arose from a power within the mechanism which ensures that any need which the organism experiences in a changing environment is met by the production of the appropriate adaptation. Which explanation is the more satisfying?'

There is of course much more to the neo-Mendelian (neo-Darwinian) viewpoint that Cannon would have us see, yet it is natural that, in the present climate of opinion, when perhaps nearly 500 papers appear every year detailing minutely the results of small-scale experiments that appear to support it, he had to overstate his case in order that his small book should attain a hearing for a doctrine so far apart from views acceptable in English-speaking biological circles. This is doubly strange for the principle of *homeostasis* to which Cannon appeals again and again has become completely respectable in our academic circles so far as physiology is concerned.

Such a doctrine of needs must accord well with Teilhard's views. Since he is concerned before all else with the rise of consciousness, it is obvious that increasing consciousness must make for increasing awareness of needs. This is certainly likely to show itself in altered behaviour which may, in certain circumstances, be the first step in the acquirement of new characters. One difficulty is certainly to see clearly what relations the Lamarckian hypothesis and the neo-Darwinian theory must bear to one another if both, as I believe, are in some sense true. This is where Teilhard helps us considerably, though (by virtue of his phraseology and the use of the 'symbiosis' – quite unnecessarily dragged in –) somewhat mistily. His vision here seems true and, with his suggestions in mind to guide us, it might be very worth while to work over some of the relevant evidence again. If the views of Darwin and Lamarck can be reconciled in this way and found operative in the interpretation of the patterns which we see in the evolution of organisms, very much indeed will have to be achieved. This seems to me an example of the germinal nature that can inhere in much of Teilhard's work and an indication of the role it may yet be seen to play in the history of science.

For many reasons it was not well or, in some quarters, even seriously, received yet nevertheless many of the arguments it put forward remain unanswered and often totally disregarded. One reason (among several) was perhaps that many committed Darwinists saw no way of reconciling its standpoints with those of the system to which they had already pledged an allegiance. The position, in fact, was probably not unlike that existing for the physicists between the conflicting implications of Quantum theory and those of the General Theory of Relativity. The importance, to me, of Teilhard's footnote cited above is that it gives us a hint about the essential nature of the reconciliation between the neo-Lamarckian and neo-Darwinian viewpoints. The essential 'anti-chance' nature of the neo-Lamarckian view appears as the 'utilisation' of Darwinian chance, the two evolutionary mechanisms being inextricably commingled together at all levels in nature. In an intuitive flash of great perspicacity Teilhard says we can see this if we distinguish between a biology of small complexes and another of great, much as we do in physics (a favourite and re-iterated analogy of his). Although the laws of both theories operate throughout nature yet the Darwinian will be found to apply more to the small and the Lamarckian more to the great. This must give an added significance to Teilhard's central theme of the rise of consciousness and, by implication, throws more light on the nature of progress in Teilhardian theory.

Yet with so much seemingly gained by adopting Teilhard's views, our difficulties are not at an end in the consideration which must be given to the views that have been held of the nature of biological progress. To make a fair exposition of this we must notice the conclusions of another group of biologists of whom Hennig[1] may well stand as a somewhat typical exponent. He says 'All progressive development from the simplest cell to the vertebrate animal and the highest type of plant can only be regarded as a pure progress *in a certain field*, and it is definitely *not* a progress towards biological perfection. The trend of evolution results in enormous complication; no biological sense can be traced in it with certainty.' This indeed is a lion in the path of our speculation! Teilhard, I suppose, would have ignored this view as untenable and unworthy and passed along believing that he would never be bitten in the rear! Others of us are more timorous.

Obviously such a viewpoint throws into relief how very subjective are these evaluations of the patterns which we believe can be demonstrated in nature. Yet this must neither cause us to reject them as vaguely 'unscientific' nor absolve us from the attempt either to see the patterns or to evolve symbolic representations of them which will make them more accessible to consciousness and the processes of rationality. Undoubtedly there is a sense, it seems to me, in which Hennig is right: there is *no* progress to perfection.[2] Yet there

[1] Hennig, E., 'Von Zwangsablauf und Geschmeidigkeit in organischer Entfaltung', *Rektoratsreden Tübingen*, No. 26, pp. 3–48 (Tübingen, 1929).

[2] This idea of the perfect type for each grade of animal and plant organisation comes down to us from the young Goethe (loc. cit.). It is difficult to see what definition we could give to the word. In terms of

is another sense in which it seems to have some meaning for us – and that one that is constantly overlooked by Teilhard. I refer to the performance of function by increased economy of means. Thus the six paired aortic arches of the primitive vertebrate are quickly reduced to four pairs in the dipnoid fish and these themselves undergo still further but *differing* reduction in reptiles, birds and mammals. The reduction therefore takes several forms and has appeared along different developmental lines in the course of evolution.[1] Teilhard stressed 'The Law of Complexification' (*Phenomenon*, p. 48) and the law of the 'fixity' of basic type. Of course, he was right in doing so, but everywhere there is a law of increasing economy of means of which he made little or nothing. Although there is no opportunity here to pursue this matter perhaps we can relate these two diverse and seemingly opposed patterns to Beurlen's[2] view that the perfection of types is due to an ever widening range of environmental stimuli (*Umwelterweiterung*) during the history of life and that this is accompanied by an increase in an autonomous structural principle called into being by 'A will to self-formation' (*Wille zur Eigengestaltung*).

Finally, in considering Teilhard's views of progress and how it is brought about in evolution, there is one other matter that must concern us, the more so because it has a bearing on the theme of social progress. This is the concept of macromutation; the belief that evolution sometimes, if rarely, takes place, not only by the infinite 'addition' of small variants moulded by natural selection, but by large-scale

---

Muller's definition of organism (*supra* footnote 2, p. 13); it would, I suppose, apply to that organism which possessed the greatest potentiality for further evolution. If, so, quite certainly it could never be estimated.

[1] Nor does this kind of evidence come from comparative morphology alone. Prof. Vachon (Vachon, M., 'The Biology of Scorpions', *Endeavour*, Vol. 12, pp. 80–89 (1953)) shows how, in adverse circumstances, scorpions can exist perfectly well with only one of their eight pairs of lungs functioning!

[2] Beurlen, K., *Die stammesgeschichtlichen Grundlagen der Abstammungslehre* (Jena, 1937).

'quanta' occurring as it were instantaneously. In a former paper I have argued this technically by considering the evolutionary patterns of the Arachnida:[1] Teilhard is not, with one exception, much concerned with this and one cannot assess his views on it with certainty. His one unequivocal statement on this matter appears to be that on page 171 of *The Phenomenon*; discussing the birth of intelligence he says 'What at first sight disconcerts us, on the other hand, is the need to accept that this step could only be achieved *at one single stroke*'. This appears to invoke something very like macromutation, a concept of considerable importance to evolution as it must, naturally, be to social progress.

Social Progress

There are possibly no clearer or more lucid passages in *The Phenomenon* than those (to be found on pp. 164–166 and pp. 245–247) in which the author argues the unique nature of Man as a consciously reflective being. Much depends upon this: the proof that life, 'like all growing magnitudes in the world' needs 'to become different so as to remain itself', and the growing awareness of mankind as a real entity and not just a vague concept, are perhaps the most important. Yet it is obvious in reading these that Teilhard has convinced himself entirely that Man is indeed separated from the animals by an apparently unbridgeable chasm: 'Admittedly the animal knows. *But it cannot know that it knows.*'

This, I think, is an argument difficult to support from what is known of animal behaviour. Professor N. J. Berrill,[2] in whose fine book most readers of Teilhard de Chardin would find much to their taste and not a little for their correction, makes the point that for every planned action 'a certain form

[1] Turk, F. A., 'Form, Size, Macromutation and Orthogenesis in the Arachnida', *Ann. Natal Mus.*, Vol. 14, pp. 1–20 (1964). It is a small irony that, if I am right in interpreting Teilhard as having a belief in Macromutation, the only instance that he gives to it – the birth of intelligence – is one that I myself would judge to be largely unaffected by macromutation!

[2] Berrill, N. J., *Man's Emerging Mind* (London, 1955).

of imagination' is necessary. The animal must, in some sense, picture itself going through this or that performance *in the future*. 'Baboon, ape and man-ape have, or had it to a marked extent; we have developed it to an extraordinary extent' (p. 76). This view is very much more in accord with fact both anatomical and psychological. The ability to project oneself into the future seems very definitely to depend upon the growth of the fore-brain. Of this we know much. This growth is in itself dependent upon the increase, over many millions of years, of the brain tissue known as the neopalium (in contra-distinction to the more primitive archaepalium represented, in part, by the brain system). The discoverer and namer of these structures, the late Sir Elliot Grafton Smith, showed very clearly the long series of ascendent evolutionary forms through which could be traced the upsurge, backward enveloping growth, and final domination of the neopalium. So complete is this evidence that morphologically there is every reason to suppose that Man's ability to reflect was of gradual emergence. L. Paul in his *Nature into History* (London, 1957), on the other hand, sees civilisation more as an 'emergent' in Lloyd Morgan's use of the term. A clear distinction must be made between the realms of nature and Man, according to Paul, because Man moves in a certain 'spiritual dimension' in which nature supplies nothing and Man must supply all. In the sense that Man must and does elaborate symbols for this, unshared by animals, it is of course true and it may be that the author's view of these difficulties will be found more logical than Teilhard's, although equally untenable in separating emergent man completely from the matrix of nature.

Now, as to the second of Teilhard's propositions, cited in the first paragraph of this section, it appears to me we are on much firmer ground and it is much to the point that he admits this to be 'a *growing* awareness'. As the American anthropologist Prof. Kluckhorn says, '. . . as men of all nations struggle to adjust themselves to the new demands of the international situation, they steadily modify their conceptions of themselves and others. Slowly but surely, a new social order and new personality trends will emerge in the process.'[1] Many of us have seen this happen, not just in our own life-times but in the last two decades! Undeniably, there is much here that supports Teilhard's views of the nature of Man and perhaps even of the emergence of a super-consciousness. This is one face of the theme of social progress.

But there is another and antithetical one, it seems to me, that is almost completely neglected by Teilhard because inconsistent with his vision of the distant horizons upon which he best loves (and needs) to dwell. This is the tendency of the human society to fractionate into ever smaller groups; nor is this solely a thing of the past or of the primitive. As an example one has only to think of the numerous sub-groups in our own technological society, each often with its own argot like that of criminals, or the members of Winchester College with its language synthesised from mediaeval latin and generations of schoolboy slang. There was a just point to Bernard Shaw's witticism, 'The Golden Rule is really: don't do unto others as you would have them do unto you – their tastes may be different'.[2] Indeed, are there not likely to be more closely defined limits to the convergence on which Teilhard placed so much emphasis and hope, and may we not just as easily see in evolution a pattern for Teilhard's super-consciousness, such that the component parts – each widely diversified – co-operate together like the different tissues of an organic body or the many castes of a termitary?[3] One cannot help thinking in this connection that

[1]Kluckhorn, C., *Mirror for Man: a survey of Human Behaviour and Social Attitudes* (New York, 1949).

[2] As a general rule contiguous groups of existing Primitives seem to have arrived at a kind of workable adjustment one with another where inter-tribal strife is reduced to a minimum; probably this has been the general rule throughout history. Outstanding evidence of what is possible is to be seen in the systems known to the anthropologist as 'dumb barter' and 'symbiotic trade' but there are many other social institutions that would as well exemplify this view of one half of the human condition.

[3] Perhaps this is indeed what Teilhard is suggesting on page 286 of *The Phenomenon*; however I have read this several times and must confess to being still uncertain as to what his standpoint is exactly. I take it that he feels it may be an advantageous thing to enter into a kind of psychic

2

Prof. Bosanquet's[1] view of the individual in relation to the Absolute, whilst having much in it that is very similar to Teilhard's, is yet more pregnant with significance for us and more justly renders the patterns we can extract from nature, in so far as he holds purpose secondary to individuality and tells us that we must understand the world, not in terms of purpose, but of the principle of individuality.

If one thing is definite in Teilhard's theories it is that civilisation is itself a great step forward to the realisation of the omega point; that social progress is real, is possible, is directional and almost that (if we believe in his philosophy) it is certain. Moreover he believes he can demonstrate all of this from the observable facts of nature. But were those facts *all* that were to be observed? For all his concern to expound his philosophy from the standpoint of evolution, one senses that he would not altogether easily have accepted a thesis such as that put forward by Desmond Morris.[2] Teilhard's fastidiousness would surely have felt this too much of the ancient ape in the old Adam.

Perhaps it is a useful corrective, providing an illuminated perspective, if we recall that not all writers have seen social progress as real, inevitable or even desirable. If such writers are seldom to the purposes of the modern state, or to the modern taste, that is possibly all the greater reason for mentioning them here. The Cambridge philosopher F. C. S. Schiller[3] early in this century had this to say: 'It appears that we can extract no guarantee of progress from the nature of man or from the nature of human institutions. . . .

---

symbiosis with minds on other planets but that any attempt on the part of Man to seek 'to fulfil himself collectively upon himself' will result in evil. If I have interpreted him here aright it seems a very curious and very considerable supposition.

[1] Bosanquet, B., *The Principle of Individuality and Value* (London, 1912.) The reader of Teilhard perhaps over-sympathetic to his views should note the very close definitions – although with wide connotations – which Bosanquet gives to individuality. This is a notable feat in Logic itself where the rule is 'the wider the denotation the vaguer the connotation'.

[2] Morris, D., *The Naked Ape* (London, 1968).

[3] Schiller, F. C. S., *Tantalus* (London, 1915).

Civilisation, as at present constituted, is very definitely a deteriorating agency, conducive to the degeneration of mankind.'

From a scholar in a different discipline comes another testimony which, even if we reject it, we should do well to think upon, especially during a reading of the last fifty odd pages of Teilhard's *Phenomenon*. Startlingly enough perhaps, T. Stärcke[1] identifies civilisation as the cause of a mental abnormality which he calls 'metaphrenia'. 'Civilisation', he says, 'from the individual point of view belongs to neurotic phenomena. . . . The civilisation of a people or a race is built up in cycles according to the mechanisms of the obsessional neurosis, until it becomes no longer bearable . . . there is a breaking through of forbidden things in war and revolution, according to the principles of the manic psychoses, while various "isms" analogous to the paranoid fields are not lacking . . . civilisation demands regression.' Those of us who have lived above half a century may well be excused if we thought we saw something to the point in this. At least these are other patterns that some thinkers have seen in nature. Whatever social progress may be, it seems to me that it is nothing if not relative – a view from which a careful reading of Teilhard's works has failed to dissuade me.

Yet, having concluded the last paragraph with such a confession, I am quite fully persuaded that Teilhard is correct in seeing that the whole course of evolution is towards 'more consciousness, more personality'. Moreover, in connection with social progress it seems to me he makes a valuable contribution in calling attention to the following properties of consciousness: (1) that it centres everything partially upon itself and (2) that it centres itself upon itself

---

[1] Stärcke, T., 'Psychoanalysis and Psychiatry', *Internat. Journ. Psycho-Anal.*, Vol. 2, pp. 361–415 (1921). It is a measure, no doubt, of how uncomfortable sociologists feel when confronted with such views as this and the last, that Sir Morris Ginsburg in his great work *Evolution and Progress* (London, 1961) makes no mention of either, nor of their several sympathisers, e.g. Roberts, M., *Malignancy and Evolution* (London, 1926), as well as some of the entomologists who have worked on the social life of insects.

constantly and increasingly.[1] That it seems impossible to reconcile these two kinds of 'pattern extraction' suggests that all the theories we have are inadequate (including Teilhard's) and that we must wait for further re-thinking of the many issues involved.

Yet in a sense it was one of Teilhard's own countrymen who provided the strongest argument against his belief in the *necessity* of social progress, and his belief that the hopes for man's future would rest on a quasi-religious faith which turns progress into a sort of god. The ends of humanity, says Renouvier, must always remain dependent on divine aid. His argument is closely reasoned and should be studied even by those, like myself, who do not accept his conclusions.[2]

Writers are not wanting, of course, who, like Teilhard, have seen an inevitable social progress which must fulfil religious or ethical ideals. Indeed theories of the same type as Teilhard's have an origin at least as old as the latter half of the eighteenth century. Thus, Prof. Ginsburg most succinctly sums up Herder's[3] reading of history: 'History is a process whereby man is slowly educated for humanity (*Erziehung zur Humanität*), that is, a process through which the qualities of *Menschlichkeit* are elicited and extended to the whole of humanity.' It might almost be a first draft of Teilhard's theory from one of his notebooks![4]

---

[1] The third of Teilhard's attributes of consciousness, viz. that of being brought by this very super-centration into association with all the other centres, is one that I cannot fully accept although I believe it is valuable to have it pointed out. Of the three social mechanisms, imitation, suggestion and sympathy, the last is, I suppose, most functional in this connection. What puzzles me is whether Teilhard is doing more than suggest, in rather florid and not very evocative language, the effect of the exercise of increasing powers of sympathy.

[2] Renouvier, A., *Essais de Critique Générale* (Paris 1864). There is a most important and critical exposition of this and other cognate views concerning social progress in Sir Morris Ginsburg's book mentioned in note 1, p. 27.

[3] Herder, J. G. von, *Ideas of the Philosophy of the History of Humanity* (Ideen zur Philosophie der Geschichte) (1784).

[4] Any reader wishing to place Teilhard's views in an historical perspective could not do better than read Prof. Bury's *The Idea of Progress*

And what other perspectives we might open up on *Teilhard's* views of social progress! How are we to see in his context and in the sweep of his vision the factual sardonic surgery of the springs of social life and its governing mechanisms, which Pareto[1] bequeathed to us: the overwhelming part played by the unthinking emotional surges in the human mind, and those irrational sentiments, beliefs, fears and ecstasies, which play the major part in shaping our social institutions?

Last, but certainly not least, in reading Teilhard's views on Man's destiny we must bear in mind all those philosophies of history which have seen no pattern, no guarantee of progress, no evidence of the perfectioning of Man at all. These are the homologues of the biological writers such as Hennig who saw in the realms of nature no evidence for the perfecting of biological types. Most typical and certainly one of the most eminent of this type of philosophical historian is Prof. H. J. Muller.[2] The seeming purpose of consciousness as Prof. Muller sees it differs somewhat from Teilhard's views: it is to produce the truly rational person – no less – one who has not merely 'good habits or right principles but one who knows what he believes and assumes the intellectual and moral responsibilities of his beliefs'. It follows that 'the best society is that which is most conducive to the growth of such persons' (p. 74). This in effect seems to be the state that Karl Popper names 'the Open Society'.[3] Such findings are

---

(1920). The effect will be salutary and will, I think, throw into relief the underlying naiveté of many of Teilhard's assumptions.

[1] Pareto, V., *The Mind and Society* (Trattato di Sociologia generale, London, 1935, 4 vols.). There can be few more testing contexts for any all-inclusive metaphysic of Teilhard's kind than to be read by an uncommitted reader fresh from studying Pareto's work especially his Vol. i, *Non-Logical Conduct*, and of that volume, especially the cruelly insistent Chapter IV, 'Theories Transcending Experience'. Its relevance extends far beyond the field of Theoretical Sociology to which it is ostensibly devoted.

[2] Muller, H. J., *The Uses of the Past* (Oxford, 1952).

[3] Popper, K., *The Open Society and its Enemies* (London, 1945).

extremely modest compared with Teilhard's for there is no hint here of a growth of super-consciousness, no 'noosphere', merely the 'complete man', or perhaps in Teilhard's terminology the completely personalised man. This is a humanist's view of the end of the evolution of the human race – its final product. Yet in Muller's view this too must pass away: '. . . if we feel that our society is damned and doomed, we can add that all great societies were sufficiently damned and were certainly doomed.' . . . but 'if all great societies have died, none is really dead. Their peoples have vanished as all men must, but first they enriched the great tradition of high enduring values' . . . so – 'we too shall vanish into the same darkness and live on in the same tradition'; thus 'we might be freed from the vanity of grandiose hopes, as of petty concerns' (p. 362).

Finally, this brings me to two points which seem to me best worth the making in putting, as I have tried to do, Teilhard's theories into a perspective that reveals and at once clarifies, tests, and perhaps diminishes. Nowhere, that I can find, in all the vast mirage of the future to which Teilhard would lead us, nor in that long pathway to the beginnings of life along which he hurries us, is there a hint of the wonder and meaning of memory. Whatever else has evolved with Man surely this is demonstrably at the heart of his progress. And yet how near this power of memory lies to Teilhard's purposes had he not wished to convince us of his 'Omega-point'! Since Proust's great novel[1] we have all been able to be aware of the possibility which memory opens to life, – the possibility of a certain 'deliverance from time' – that time which has shackled all other species to the inevitabilities of its own passage. How closely this conforms with some of Teilhard's views about us may be glimpsed in the following passage from the philosopher Santayana.[2] Only transpose such terms in it as 'reflective', 'intelligent' and 'apprehension' with those

[1] Proust, M., *A La Recherche du Temps Perdu* Eng. trans. 'Remembrance of Things Past', (Chatto & Windus, 12 vols.).

[2] Santayana, G., *The Life of Reason*. Vol. 3, 'Reason in Religion' (London, 1905). The quotation is from pp. 262–263.

of Teilhard's system and you will see the point: 'Ever since substance became at some sensitive point intelligent and reflective, ever since time made room and pause for memory, for history, for the consciousness of time, a god, as it were, became incarnate in mortality and some vision of truth, some self-forgetful satisfaction, became a heritage that moment could transmit to moment and man to man. . . . To participate in this vision is to participate at once in humanity and divinity, since all other bonds are material and perishable, but the bond between two thoughts that have grasped the same truth, of two instants that have caught the same beauty, is a spiritual and imperishable bond.'

To many of us this will seem a more demonstrable pattern than that which Teilhard eventually produces and moreover one derived from much the same range of facts. To most who feel this, it will seem a persistent sadness that finally he fails so far and by so much. As for the cause of his failure, it is perhaps inherent in the nature of his task. The whole history of the type of Christian apologetics based on science is an unfortunate and embarrassing one. Very few among its practitioners have been able to deal anything but tendentiously with either the one or the other – or both! Possibly the most successful have been the scientific neo-Thomists of whom A. Gemelli in his many papers in the *Rivista di filosofice neo-scholastica* (Milan 1909 onwards) was one of the most distinguished. Yet even he wilts under the strain. It is a marked characteristic of such writings – and a curious one – that they proceed either by 'watering down' today's physics or 'thickening up' yesterday's biology!

Perhaps, in this respect, the older writers, such as some of those of the Bridgewater treatises, did better with the science of their times; but for all his competence, erudition, sincerity and charm, a writer like William Kirby ('On the Powers, Wisdom and Goodness of God as manifested in the Creation of Animals and in their History, Habits, and Instincts,' London 1835, 2 vols., being Volume 7 of the Bridgewater Treatises) would provide but a vaporous basis for any scientific demonstration of theism. All writers who base a system of Christian apologetics on the mutabilities of science seem to hold particularly *jejune* views of this history of science – not excepting Teilhard himself. It is strange that such writers have not made more use, as a base for their arguments, of Vaihinger's theory of fictions (Vaihinger, *The Philosophy of 'As If'*, London, 1924), a book that Teilhard could surely never have read!

A theism it seems may be experienced or even explained but it cannot be demonstrated from that same groundwork of nature with which the biologist or physicist deals. It is a pity that so many writers seem to have felt that this essentially invalidates it.

But there exists a greater and wholly ineradicable reason for the failure of Teilhard's system as it presents itself in the theme of progress. It is this: anyone who would erect an all inclusive metaphysic solely on the real or imagined ground-work of evolution and the assumption of the 'primacy of matter' must have an intellect, however exalted, flawed in some measure with '*hubris*'. Teilhard's failure is basically and fatally a lack of the essential intellectual humility that there must be to accept the relativism with which all ideas of such an order are forever and essentially tinged. And to this there must be added his extremely naïve ideas about the nature of science and its relation to actuality; just how naïve these ideas must be will be demonstrated to any one reading Cassirer's work. Yet, because he gives us, as it were, one more in a plurality of definitions of nature – all of which add a little to the scope of our insights into natural phenomena – we shall forgive him these failings if only because it is to our own advantage to do so – or even, perhaps, because they are, in a measure, equally our own.

TWO

Teilhard: Analogy and Dialectic

A. O. DYSON

'While the normal approach of thought to a static reality is to *enclose* ideas in a continually more general idea, to include them in a continually wider theory, in which they appear as particular cases, to arrange them in a logical structure, the expression of a history of progress calls for an original method that brings out the relation between being and becoming' (Rideau). 'In Teilhard there is analogy everywhere. But what sort of analogy is it? . . . The effort to achieve a little rigour means the loss of literary charm. In Teilhard, what is gained in charm is balanced by what is lost in rigour' (Grenet). [1] . . . The Teilhardian dialectic, apart from which no understanding of his work is possible' (Barthélemy-Madaule).

These three quotations set the scene for an attempt, in this short essay, to try and determine exactly where the main critical issue in Teilhard's thought in fact lies. Such a clarification is certainly necessary in view of the frequent, diverse and still unresolved discussion which Teilhard's *œuvre* has evoked in the last decade – not least among scientists, philosophers and theologians.

By and large three main trends of criticism can be discerned. (1) There are the critics who have judged Teilhard's writings to be worthy of extended examination. After such

[1] Grenet, Paul-Bernhard, *Pierre Teilhard de Chardin ou le philosophe malgré lui* (Paris 1960).

careful scrutiny some theologians have suggested that, at a number of points, Teilhard's scheme stands in serious and irreconcilable opposition to traditional Christian belief. Likewise, after careful study some scientists have felt bound to conclude that in Teilhard's enterprise scientific rigour is, at certain vital points, replaced by fragile speculation. (2) There are the critics who have quickly dismissed Teilhard's *œuvre* as fundamentally too muddle-headed to deserve any serious consideration at all. (3) Between these two positions there is a solid middle ground of critics who remain both convinced and unconvinced. The same can also be said of many general readers who do not feel disposed to reject Teilhard out of hand, but who also have neither the time nor the skill to carry out a detailed analysis of his writings. Many such readers would judge that, in their study of works by and about Teilhard, they have indeed journeyed with an adventurous and imaginative spirit. At the same time they feel compelled to entertain – even if they cannot adequately explain – a definite sense of misgiving which cannot be lightly set aside. It is as if Teilhard's thought, often so impressive in its parts, is none the less as a whole shot through by a major flaw. Has not Teilhard, at the end of the day, fallen victim to a general confusion of thought? Has he treated with sufficient seriousness those real and abiding distinctions which must be drawn between different areas of life and modes of thought if intellectual, moral and religious integrity is to be preserved? Has he not, in a word, laid claim to a synthesis where there is no synthesis and thereby quite improperly blurred the autonomies which belong to natural science, religion, philosophy, sociology, etc.? I would judge that this is indeed the chief issue raised by Teilhard's *œuvre*, and that there is perhaps not much to be gained from an examination of more detailed aspects of his thought unless this main issue can be clarified and unless Teilhard's defence against such a charge can be seen to be what it is.

In these few pages I shall do no more than try to set this enquiry in motion along what I believe to be the appropriate lines. I must leave many major issues unresolved. But at least I hope to show how Teilhard undertook their resolution and thereby define more precisely the points at which criticism of his work can most usefully continue. It is to my mind altogether remarkable that among the countless studies devoted to Teilhard's *œuvre*, only a handful have given any sustained attention to that feature of his thought which provides the clue to the questions posed in the previous paragraph. I refer to the notion of *dialectic*. It is this notion above all that must be examined and evaluated if the pattern and the direction of Teilhard's thought are to be clearly grasped. In some respects the critical silence over Teilhard's dialectic can be understood if not excused. For to some extent Teilhard's account of dialectic lies below the surface of his writings, to emerge explicitly only from time to time. Nevertheless the clues to this notion of dialectic abound on nearly every page of Teilhard's *œuvre* from the earliest essays to the latest. In this respect, students of Teilhard stand in the debt of two scholars who have fastened upon the notion of dialectic and have given to it the prominence which it deserves in Teilhard's thought. I refer to Claude Cuénot and to Madeleine Barthélemy-Madaule. In the case of Cuénot attention should be drawn especially to an article entitled *Situation de Teilhard de Chardin*.[1] In the case of Barthélemy-Madaule, the reader is pre-eminently directed to the thirty or so pages which form the introduction to her volume *La Personne et le drame humain chez Teilhard de Chardin*. Betraying a profound acquaintance with, and understanding of, Teilhard's writings, the author examines the sources of Teilhard's dialectic, its implicit use in *The Phenomenon of Man*, and its explicit formulation in some of Teilhard's later writings.

At the outset Madaule observes that it is in fact impossible to speak of the *sources* of Teilhard's dialectic in the usual sense of philosophical ancestors. Thus Teilhard may not be read, for example, in an hegelian or marxist perspective. At the same time there are certain features common to dialectical

[1] Cuénot, Claude. 'Situation de Teilhard de Chardin', *Bulletin de la Société Industrielle de Mulhouse*, no. 3. 1963.

thinking which Teilhard shares. 'Dialectic is movement; but not all movement is dialectical. Dialectic is a movement of thought; but not every movement of thought is dialectical. In opposition to the unilinear process of deduction or induction in its traditional forms . . ., there stands an operation which takes account of a plurality. . . .'[1] Unilinear reasoning is concerned solely to avoid the false and to pursue the true, whereas dialectical reasoning reveals that the way to truth is not straight and simple but passes through the vicissitudes of antitheses and mediations. Dialectical movement engenders novelty without breaking a coherent continuity. The general sense of dialectic suggests therefore a notion of becoming in which movement occurs through the confrontation of manifold opposites or differences; the notion of synthesis; the notion of a novelty concurrent with necessity; and the notion of a totality.

Teilhard's own treatment of dialectic has its roots in an attitude and a conviction which can be discerned in some of his earliest essays. The defining and characteristic feature of his thought is *conflict*. Reality too (and the 'too' I shall refer to again) is above all marked by conflict, is seen as a multiplicity which we must overstep and overcome. We can only attain to a synthesis between belief in God and belief in the world if we reject a static conjunction of the two and envisage instead an outcome in which the two have converged after each undergoing a mutation or 'creative transformation'. These oppositions are not merely 'thought through'; they are lived out in a personal drama of the spirit. '. . . Conflicts, oppositions, separations, forward movements of synthesis, oppositions which emerge again out of a provisional synthesis . . . – enough of a positive nature for us to proceed, for us to hope and to build; enough recurrent negativity to ensure that movement never ceases.'[2]

From the first we discern this analogy between 'reality' and the 'act of the spirit'. The spirit is engaged in a process

[1] Madaule, *La Personne et le drame humain chez Teilhard de Chardin.* Editions du Seuil. Paris 1967, p. 15.
[2] Madaule, p. 19.

of unification which is never complete; the universe is seen as a 'creative union', as a 'struggle against the multitude', i.e. a diversity which is overcome by the emergence of new centres which are unforeseeable in advance but which, retrospectively, maintain coherence with what went before. This basic analogy is developed and expounded in *The Phenomenon of Man*.

'I have chosen man as the centre, and around him I have tried to establish a coherent order between antecedents and consequences (p. 29).' But in what sense is man the centre? For Teilhard man 'the centre of perspective, is at the same time the *centre of construction* of the universe' (p. 33). This means that the 'centre of perspective constituted by our consciousness is able to order the world in such a way that the convergence of lines about us is not only "visual" but "structural".'[1] It is clear that Teilhard does not wish to distinguish in any sharp way between the cognitive order and the order of reality. The subject, in seeking to transcend the universe, finds himself incorporated within it. Thus he writes, 'This duality of the cognitive order and the order of the real has always seemed to me . . . arbitrary and false. We have no serious reason for thinking that things are not made with the same rhythm as that with which our experience unfolds them.'[2] Thus the act of knowing, or seeing (the words are interchangeable), is an act of construction in which we are involved in the infinite mediations between subject and object, object and subject; in which we are involved in processes of creative union. As we should expect there is no suggestion that there are easy and simple processes. The dialectic is complex, costly, laborious; the provisional syntheses are always under permanent correction.

It is important to emphasise this. For Teilhard has often been accused of holding to notions of 'simple progress' of 'naïve optimism'. On the contrary, man as the centre of perspective and as the centre of construction is bound to, and

---

[1] Madaule, p. 20.
[2] Rideau, p. 238. *Teilhard de Chardin. A Guide to his Thought* (Collins, 1967).

at the centre of, a struggling creative union – a union deeply inserted in, and grappling with, biological reality. Indeed life so viewed can take on a deeply tragic aspect which threatens to engulf both faith in the world and faith in God. Teilhard appears to have no illusions in this respect. He speaks of the '. . . *wretched* crust of every shape and every physical property' and of the 'separation and antagonism of the elements of the cosmos'.[1]

At the same time we can also see how Teilhard's dialectic possesses a thoroughly evolutionary character. And it is in this context that he feels able to press analogy far beyond its usual limits. 'I believe that one can push the theory of analogy further in an evolutionary Universe than in a static world-structure.'[2] The key to this extended use of analogy lies then with the notion of 'creative transformation'. De Lubac describes this as 'one of the central and most constant sources of Teilhardian dialectic'.[3] This notion enables us to discern a single movement which contains both transformation and creation, continuity and novelty. We are licensed to employ analogy in such an evolutionary world-view since, in that world, 'everything is formed by transformation of a pre-existing analogue'.[4]

I do not propose to take the discussion further into the phase of Teilhard's dialectic by which he passes from Omega as a speculative point of convergence to Omega as a real and pre-existent source of all energy. But from what I have already said, some conditions to be observed in the use of theological themes can be laid down. While, by definition, the many aspects of the dialectic represent real differences, on the other hand we must be careful about the way in which we ascribe 'univocal value' to any one aspect. Such a procedure could easily lose sight of the *movement* in the dialectic. Moreover, and again by definition, the interrelations

[1] Rideau, p. 345.
[2] de Lubac, *The Faith of Teilhard de Chardin* (Burns and Oates 1965), p. 172.
[3] de Lubac, p. 173.
[4] de Lubac, p. 172.

between different aspects of reality never remain the same; they are always in process of separation, unification, and transformation. This is very important for our under-standing of the so-called data of Christian revelation. For such data refer to aspects and presuppositions of a cosmos engaged in a process of 'creative transformation'. Thus these data refer, in the language of faith, to the past, present and future of this process. Talk about faith must therefore be planted firmly in the context of man as the centre of perspec-tive and the centre of construction. There is at every moment in time a real danger that we lapse into a static mode of seeing so very different from Teilhard's *voir*, which is con-structive in character. On Teilhard's dynamic account of knowing and being, faith is always the appropriate attitude. This is finely expressed in some notes taken by Cuénot at one of Teilhard's lectures. 'There is no Christian philosophy, as if there were two opposed entities. Faith is born only of faith. It is not a case of faith on one side and reason on another. Higher and higher acts of faith: the world has a meaning – this meaning is spirit – this meaning is formed by unification – adherence to Christianity.'[1] This is not to say that there is no difference between these levels of faith, for difference there must be – but a difference which is subject to creative transformation, to the maintenance of continuity and to the emergence of novelty.

In all this, therefore, one must return to the point made earlier that Teilhard's dialectic is a lived dialectic. It is moreover a dialectic in which no breach may be effected between knowing and being, and thus a dialectic which forces upon us the fact that both our knowing and being are incomplete. Precisely by taking evolution so seriously Teilhard can insist that both the completeness and the unity of our knowledge must await, and must co-operate in bringing about, the completeness and unity of the divine milieu at and beyond Omega. Our recourse to analogy manifests, therefore, on the one hand, the real brokenness, multiplicity and tragedy of the biological space-time which man inhabits,

[1] *Nouveau Lexique Teilhard de Chardin.* p. 95. Editions du Seuil. 1968.

but also on the other hand the real drive towards unification which belongs to the cosmos. 'The main concept which illuminates [creative transformation] is the unitive act. The life which animates it is that of charity, of love. But it is a relentless love which only agrees to unite that which has passed through the fires of oppositions, of struggle, of destructions and rebirths, of deaths and resurrections.'[1]

In my view these considerations only serve to heighten the problematic nature of Teilhard's enterprise. At the same time his handling of analogy and dialectic serve, to my mind, to put paid to the objection that Teilhard has capitulated to a facile conjunction of disparate ideas. On the contrary he has outlined a standpoint which can only be tested, not by thought alone, but by thought-action in the world. The test lies, therefore, in our own lived experience, and that experience bears all the marks of incompleteness. The decision to embark constructively upon this dialectical existence depends, it would seem, upon the quality and content of one's motivation *vis-à-vis* the human future. Teilhard's motivation in this respect sprang, without any shadow of doubt, from a Christian belief which stands or falls by its convictions about the future. Whether those who do not espouse Christian belief can or do discover a profound motivation for the future, without which Teilhard's scheme is incredible, is another question. Teilhard certainly took the view that a full-blooded account of the phenomenon of man, past, present and possible future, could, quite apart from Christian belief, mightily stimulate such a motivation.

[1] Madaule, p. 46 f.

THREE

God and Evolutive Creation

R. B. SMITH

Although it has become fairly common for contemporary theologians to pay tribute to the influence of Teilhard de Chardin, recent discussion of the doctrine of God shows surprisingly few traces of his influence. The reasons for this are not far to seek. Chief among them is the fact that the starting point of most theologians is not that of Teilhard. They have learned not to divorce the doctrine of God from the doctrine of man, and in so doing some have come to confuse theology with anthropology. Teilhard, on the other hand, connects the doctrine of God not only with anthropology but with our knowledge of creation as a whole. Since the world is evolutionary in nature, he says, 'God is no longer conceivable (either structurally or dynamically) except in the measure that, like a sort of "formal" cause, he coincides (without being confounded) with the centre of convergence of cosmogenesis.'[1] That is, theology can no longer proceed as if God were 'structurally detached from his work', but the doctrine of God and the doctrines of creation and eschatology must be developed together, and ought not to be separated from science. At the same time, the doctrine of God does not derive either from science or from the doctrine of creation. God is not one natural phenomenon among others, and he cannot be known in the way we discover phenomena. While Teilhard points out that his interpretation

[1] 'Le Dieu de l'Evolution', in *Cahiers Teilhard de Chardin*, Vol. VI (Seuil, 1968), p. 14. My translation.

of evolution shows that it requires something beyond itself
for its completion and for its very existence, he also says that
what this is we must discover through some other means of
knowledge than the purely natural,[1] and maintains that
science cannot discover God.[2] *All* that he says about God
comes primarily from his faith as a Christian. Teilhard's
religious thought must not be seen as an extension of his
evolutionary ideas: it would be closer to the truth to say that
his evolutionary perspective is an extension of his faith in the
Incarnation.[3]

In exploring some of the issues which the theory of
evolutive creation raises for our understanding of God, we
must keep in mind this dual setting of the doctrine of God.
On the one hand, our knowledge of God comes from God,
above all from his self-revelation in Jesus Christ. On the
other hand, we must not make the mistake of supposing that
we can think of God apart from the world. As the world's
Omega, God is not to be found apart from the beginning,
ongoing, and end of creation.

Although he mentions it only rarely, Teilhard lays great
stress on that most distinctive of Christian beliefs about God,
the doctrine of the Trinity. God is able to create, he says,
because God himself is not a static unity but a dynamic
Trinity, that is, because God himself exists in uniting, he also
creates through a process of union[4]. If God were a simple
numerical unity, Teilhard continues, the only way he could
create would be by transforming himself into something else,
and so there is the alternative of Trinitarianism or Pantheism. But a pantheism which equates God and the universe
must be rejected both because of the revelation of God in
Christ and also because it would not satisfy the requirements

[1] 'Science and Christ', in *Science and Christ* (Collins, 1968), p. 33: 'I
would never dream, my friends, of deducing Christian dogma solely
from an examination of the properties our reason attributes to the
structure of the world.'

[2] *Ibid.*, p. 36: 'By itself, science cannot discover Christ, but Christ
satisfies the yearnings that are born in our hearts in the school of science.'

[3] See 'My Universe', in *Science and Christ*, p. 53.

[4] *Introduction à la vie chrétienne* (unpublished).

of evolution, which demand a *transcendent* Omega. On these grounds, Teilhard stresses the practical relevance of the doctrine of the Trinity.

The chief contribution of Teilhard's thought to the doctrine of God is fairly well known from *The Phenomenon of Man* and *The Future of Man*, in which he provides grounds for the belief that evolution is not yet finished but will continue to develop to higher states of personality. But this can happen only if there is something beyond evolution, a transcendent and personalising Omega, identified by faith with God, ultimately responsible for evolution. The Christian concept of God, in its turn, is greatly enlivened and enriched through being identified with the natural goal of human action and aspiration. To express it in Teilhard's own terms, he provides a synthesis of Christian faith and natural aspirations, of the 'God above' of traditional Christian belief and the 'God ahead', the natural summit of evolution, of the humanist. However, there are other contributions of Teilhard to the doctrine of God which are not so obvious. He raises questions about God for philosophy and theology which are extremely difficult to answer, but which are nevertheless very important, and must be recognised and understood. Action requires a foundation in thought, and so questions which may appear to be purely theoretical are often found to have considerable practical importance. Then too, when we find some theoretical foundations for human action, the theory is bound to raise further problems for the action. The two are inseparably bound together, and this is certainly true of questions concerning God.

In particular, it is Teilhard's attempt to sketch a 'metaphysics of union' that raises questions concerning God and an evolutionary creation. Teilhard himself formulates them to a certain extent, but others are certain to arise from any attempt to think theologically on the basis of his writings. In general, Teilhard seems to raise as many questions as he answers. With regard to the doctrine of God, his ideas raise more questions than they answer, but at the same time they provide suggestions for answers which may well prove to be more fertile and more coherent with the total structure of human knowledge than any previous ones. The aim of this essay is to undertake a preliminary exploration of questions which require a much more detailed investigation, to try to recognise the questions which should be asked and to attempt to pose them in terms of Teilhard's system. Although there are many different aspects of the doctrine of God, we shall consider at the present time only one, the relationship between God as Trinity and the beginning, development, and end of creation understood as evolution. But first it is necessary to sketch briefly the theory which Teilhard described variously as 'evolutive creation', 'creative transformation', and 'creative evolution'.[1]

Creation, Teilhard says, is not the production of a world fully made in some primordial moment, nor yet is it the bringing into existence of 'being', which changes and develops but is fully created to begin with. On the contrary, creation is an action in which God brings things into existence through the process of union which we call evolution. This is at once a continuous process and a genuine 'creation', in that it produces not merely new forms of being with each new union but also more being. Where there is no union at all there is nothingness, and God himself, perfect union, is the fullness of being. Between these two poles, himself and nothingness, God brings being into existence through union. In fact, Teilhard defines 'being' itself in terms of union, basing his definition on the combined evidence of organic evolution and the doctrine of the Trinity.

A 'Trinitarian Reflection'

Teilhard never disputed the traditional teaching of the Church that God creates *ex nihilo*. Despite some critics to the contrary,[2] Teilhard states emphatically that God does not

---

[1] On this theory see especially 'The Struggle Against the Multitude' and 'Creative Union', in *Writings in Time of War* (Collins, 1968), and 'My Universe' in *Science and Christ*. An unpublished writing, *Comment je vois*, gives a later (1948) statement of the same theory.

[2] E.g. Robert North, 'Teilhard and the Problem of Creation', *Theological Studies*, XXIV (1963), 601.

create from a portion of his own being or from any pre-existent matter.[1] God creates being, both matter and spirit, by a process of union. But if we agree that God creates out of nothing by means of union, we must ask what is the nature of the 'nothing' from which he creates. The question is not just a play on words. When it has to do with creation, particularly if we accept the theory that God creates through uniting and the definition of being in terms of union, then the question of the nature of nothingness is a very real question.

First of all, we must point out that nothingness is in the same evolutionary series as being. At each stage of evolution God brings into existence something which is more than the sum of the components which entered into the union. That is, he brings about more being, being which was not there before, from a relative nothingness. Absolute nothingness is the complete absence of any union, *total* disunion.[2] This condition Teilhard calls the 'Multiple' or 'Multitude', and he regards it as the starting-point of creation, the nothingness from which creation begins. But because it is in the same series as being, it must in some sense have a positive nature, or at least be capable of being thought in some positive manner. In fact we may go further and suggest that if the whole movement of creation from total disunity through evolution to union with God at the Omega point is a single coherent organic growth, then it must be possible to find in the Multiple not only a positive element but even something of God's nature, some trace of the Blessed Trinity. Now, if the Multiple, which is nothing, is in the same evolutionary series as being and thus must have at least the capacity for being described in a positive manner, we must ask how it came to be (insofar as it may properly be said to 'be'). Where did God find, or how did he make, the nothingness from which he creates? This also is a proper question, given

[1] See 'Action and Activation', in *Science and Christ*, p. 180.
[2] Cf. Étienne Gilson, *The Christian Philosophy of Saint Augustine* (Gollancz, 1961), p. 211: '. . . pure multiplicity, which in its extreme condition would be identical with nothingness.'

the Teilhardian frame of thought. It is a problem that bothered Teilhard, and to which he returned many times to consider it from slightly different points of view. Strangely enough, in view of his stress on the importance for creation of the fact that God is Triune, he does not seem to have considered the doctrine of the Trinity in connection with the origin of the Multiple, and it is here that we shall now look.

Might it not be worth while asking whether the origin of the Multiple is not a sort of "Trinitarian reflection'? Teilhard interprets the doctrine of the Trinity, quite rightly, to mean that there is within the Godhead a total self-giving of each of the three Persons to each of the others in love. This does not mean that there is any diminishment as a result of self-giving; there is rather an enhancement of each Person, as there is in any creative union. The union which is perfect in love brings enrichment rather than diminishment, distinction of Persons rather than confusion. The same thing can be seen on the human level, and Teilhard uses the example of the love of man and woman: a man, he points out, is never so much himself, and a wife never so much herself, as when they love each other.[1] So also we may understand that the self-giving of the Persons of the Trinity does not lead to their confusion but to their distinction. Now is not the appearance of the Multiple, to use a necessary temporal metaphor, essentially the same sort of act? Teilhard speaks of the end of creation, the Pleroma, as being 'the fruit, in some way, of a reflection of God, no longer in Himself but beyond Himself'.[2] Would it not be correct to say the same thing of all stages of creation, the beginning as well as the end? The appearance of the Multiple is another act of God's self-giving, having the same pattern as the self-giving of each divine Person to the others, a self-giving which extends throughout creation and which demands a response. When God is All, before creation has begun, there is simply no

[1] 'The Eternal Feminine' in *Writings in Time of War*, pp. 194–196; 'Esquisse d'un univers personnel', in *L'Activation de l'Energie* (Seuil, 1962), p. 91.
[2] *Comment je vois* (unpublished). My translation.

'room' for a Multiple unless and until God wills it. Therefore, in order to create from nothing, God must first give himself in order to make room for a nothingness from which he can create. He must abandon his own exclusiveness and give himself for the nothingness, so that creation may start and grow from it. This self-giving, like that within the Trinity, is not the donation of possessions which leads to their decrease, but a giving of oneself, which (speaking metaphorically, for perfection cannot be increased) makes God even more himself. A *néant créable* can only be a reflection of the Trinity, the exact opposite of God's own perfect union, and yet, because it is the recipient of God's self-giving, having a trace of union and a tendency towards union.

The question of how we can discern the trace of the Trinity in the beginning of creation is actually part of a much larger question: how can the Trinitarian structure of creation, in all its stages, be distinguished? If we regard creation, as I believe we must, as one way in which God the Blessed Trinity reveals himself *as Trinity*, that is, as uniting love, then we have to ask how the Triune nature of God is shown in creation, not only at its beginning but in its continuation and at its end. Just as Teilhard finds the pattern of the future by extrapolating from evolution past and present, so also when we are searching for the beginning of creation we find that it can be described only by extrapolation backwards by analogy from the same process of evolution. We cannot find God or discover anything about God's methods of creation by looking at the past alone, but only by seeing past, present, and future together as continuous parts of the same movement. Let us then look at the ongoing of creation, and attempt to find there the pattern of the Trinity, before we turn back to the beginnings of creation.

In evolution from matter to life to man, and the continuing evolution of mankind, we find that the means of advance is union. Union, Teilhard says, both identifies and differentiates those elements which enter into it. Now in the movement of union itself there is a reflection of the Trinity, for God exists in uniting. Referring back again to the doctrine of the

Trinity, if God is Three in One this means that the Persons
of the Trinity exist in giving themselves to each other in
union in such a way that they become at one and the same
time both totally identified with each other and totally
differentiated from each other. Within the being of God there
is union which differentiates and which is itself creative love.
The fact that what we might call the 'historical' part of
creation evolves by the same type of union, although the
difference and identity in any created union cannot be
called 'total', is a faint reflection of the life of God himself,
an 'image' of God in the universe he is creating. It is because
of the evolution of creation from nothingness to union with
God, and the fact that this takes place by a movement of the
same kind as that of God himself, that it is possible for
created beings to discover anything about God or even that
he exists. It is union which is the foundation of all analogical
reasoning, necessary not only for comparison of different
levels of evolution but also for speech about God and
creation, for the union which produces this world is above all
a distinctive characteristic of God himself.

I have more to suggest later about the end of creation,
but for the present let us say with Teilhard that creation is
the process whereby God builds up a body for his Christ.
The end of creation is the transformation of the products of
evolution, spiritual beings, into the matter of Christ. Christ
is to be identified, by the laborious work of evolution through
the ages, with the ultimate summit of evolution.[1] The
Omega point becomes finally Christ-Omega, and God's act
of creation is seen as basically his willing that his co-eternal
Son be both God and Man.

If he is the goal of creation, Christ must also be associated
in some way with its beginning. He is the one 'through whom
all things were made'. Since Omega is the moving force of
creation, it must be in his role as Omega that Christ is the
agent of creation, something of him must be present and
operative from the beginning. It is through the building up
of 'no-being' into the Body of Christ that God the Father

[1] 'Le Dieu de l'Evolution', *Cahiers* VI, 17.

creates. Teilhard expresses it as follows:

'[God] willed his Christ – and in order to have his Christ, he had to create the spiritual world, and man in particular, upon which Christ might germinate – and to have man, he had to launch the vast process of organic life (which, accordingly, is not a superfluity but an essential organ of the world); and the birth of that organic life called for the entire cosmic turbulence.'[1]

So the Father is willing his Christ, and the creation is building up into a 'cosmic body' for Christ. Here we see again the work of God as Trinity in the origin of creation.

Let us turn now to the motive force of creation, to see whether this provides further light by which we can distinguish the trace of God as Trinity. Once we have arrived at a consideration of man, it is possible to see where the motive force for the continuation of evolution comes from. It comes in part from free human response to the pressures of the environment, and it comes in part from the attractive force of the Omega, recognised by man as the goal of his evolution. But before man, what provides the push or pull that brings about evolutionary advance? What, in particular, is the attraction that begins the process of union? When all is disunity, where does the tendency to unite come from? Is God's attraction from ahead sufficient to bring about the start of creation from the Multiple, or is there some characteristic of creation, found even in the pure Multiple itself, that makes union possible under certain conditions? Teilhard was well aware of this problem, and suggested certain lines of approach. In addition to this, we may also find a second possible answer in the idea of the divine self-giving which has already been mentioned.

In some of his early writings Teilhard raised the question of the 'universal element': is there some 'element' found throughout creation which makes union possible?[2] He

[1] 'My Universe', in *Science and Christ*, p. 79.
[2] See especially, 'Note on the Universal Element', pp. 271–276, and 'The Universal Element', pp. 289–302, in *Writings in Time of War*.

suggests that the universal element, present in every particle of being, is 'the penetrating influence of Christ-Omega' (an attraction from ahead?). Again, he suggests that it is 'the Will of God, conceived as a special energy instilled into beings to animate them and order them towards their end'. Or, again, it is 'God's creative action' – but if our question concerns the nature of God's creative action, this is not very helpful. Finally, Teilhard concludes that the real universal element is the 'cosmic influence of Christ'. It is difficult to take exception to any of these suggested answers, but none really comes to grips with our question. What is it in creation, and what is it in the 'nothingness', which makes possible the production of being through union, especially when we recognise that evolution is not a simple straight-line movement, a development of what already existed into new and higher forms, but the coming into existence of new being from nothingness by creative union?

It is possible to take these suggestions of Teilhard and interpret them theologically to refer to the indwelling presence of God the Holy Spirit. Would it not be possible to say that the motive force in creative union is the presence of the Holy Spirit, God immanent in creation and active even in the pre-material Multitude? The 'penetrating influence of Christ-Omega' is surely the Spirit of Christ. The 'Will of God', active in all beings and causing them to develop towards the goal of personal union with God, is surely the Spirit of God. We may say then that God the Holy Spirit is the reason why it is possible for union to take place, for being to come from no-being, for the Multiple to respond to the attraction from ahead of Omega. In traditional theology the Holy Spirit is regarded both as the bond of union between the Father and the Son, and thus the function of uniting is already attributed to him, and also as the one through whose action Christ is born. Therefore we may say that creation mirrors the life of the Trinity insofar as in both it is the Spirit that is the principle of union, the 'bond of love divine', who makes possible a true 'creative union'. We may say also that whenever Christ is born he is 'conceived

by the Holy Ghost', who works through matter to bring to
birth Christ's cosmic body, just as through the Blessed Virgin
Mary he brought about the physical birth of Jesus Christ.
We are therefore justified in attributing to the Holy Spirit
the tendency within the material universe for the elements to
seek a goal, to move in a certain direction through union. It
is he, together with the attraction of God-Omega, the goal
ahead, who provides the motive force that enables union to
take place and creation to come out of nothingness.

The other possible approach, which should not replace
the previous suggestion but may be taken together with it,
has to do with the action of God as Trinity in limiting
himself to pose a nothingness from which he might create.
As we have already seen, this act must be similar to the
relations of the Persons within the Trinity. As the Father,
Son and Holy Spirit in giving themselves to each other are
both totally identified in the union and totally differentiated,
completely one and yet definitely three, so also when God
as Trinity gives himself to produce a multiple from which
he can by union make a creation, he must in some sense
become both identified with this nothingness – although not
entirely, since at the beginning the giving is entirely one-
sided – and differentiated from it. The same relationship in
miniature must exist between God and the universe, with
the reservation just mentioned, as between the three Persons
in the Trinity. They are both the same and different: God
is one with his creation, yet God is God and creation is
creation and the two must never be confused; God is present
in creation, and yet God is apart from creation and 'wholly
other'. This means, surely, that within the Multiple, as
within all the stages of creation, there is a replica of the self-
giving nature of the Trinity, put there by the very act of
God's posing the nothingness to begin with, and that this
makes possible unions which differentiate a creative advance.

A Pattern of Self-giving
We now turn to examine questions of a somewhat different type,
of more immediate practical concern than the preceding

ones. That is not to say that they are not theological, or
that the ones we have been thinking of do not have profound
practical implications. What we shall do now is look at some
of the same problems but ask slightly different questions
about them, questions which have to do specifically with
human action.

Let us look again at the question of how creation proceeds.
What makes it work, what makes the process of evolution go
on as it does? Ordinary simple development is quite straight-
forward, but what is it that causes the changes that occur
at what Teilhard calls 'critical points', so that life appears
where there was no life and thought where there was no
thought? In *The Phenomenon of Man*, Teilhard argues that
because we know that consciousness exists in man as a
characteristic property, it must have an extension throughout
the universe, not of course in the same form as it occurs in
man, but in the sense that it is correct to speak of the
'Within' of creation as a whole, even though the nature of
the 'Within' is not the same at any two levels of evolution.
Is it not equally valid to argue that since in man evolution
becomes 'self-evolution', there is a cosmic extension of this
as well? This does not mean that atoms are also self-evolutive,
or that anything lower than man can properly be said to be
self-evolutive, but it does mean that we ought to recognise
that there is an element of freedom or spontaneity, or something analogous to this, throughout evolution. That is, the
'Within', however slightly developed, is not inert but has a
part in determining the response of the element to external
pressure. Perhaps this is what Huxley meant when he
referred, in a rather peculiar phrase, to evolution as pro-
ceeding by means of the 'basic biological facts of self-repro-
duction, mutation and selection, with perhaps a little
orthogenesis added.'[1] What Huxley seems to mean is that
when the external pressures and the internal chemico-
physical reactions have all been taken into account, something else, which can only come from the 'Within', is still
necessary to account for the way evolution has progressed.

[1] *The New Systematics* (Oxford, 1940), p. 11.

This, I suggest, is an element of 'self-evolution', not the same as human self-evolution but organically connected with it in the same series, and at the lower levels so small as to be almost, but not quite, non-existent.

This interpretation of *The Phenomenon of Man* is not intended to replace what I said a short while ago about the Holy Spirit as the agent that acts from within creation to create. Rather, I think the two must be held together. It is true that God's initiative in creation is the most important thing. God creates, creation does not make itself. Yet it is also true that God depends on the response of his creation in order to create. This has to do again with the idea of self-giving. God gives up himself to pose a 'nothingness' from which to create. But in order for there to be creation, the image or trace of the Trinity that is within the nothingness must respond, both through the active presence in it of the Holy Spirit and also to some extent (and at the initial stages it must be to a very small extent indeed) of its own free will.

Much the same considerations apply with regard to human evolution. The 'self-evolutive' nature of creation has come explicitly to the fore in man. As Teilhard never ceases to stress, the future of creation is up to us. The universe itself must be such that evolution can continue beyond its present stage in man as far as the Omega point, at which all that is of value in evolution, the human person especially, will find lasting security. But still the future is not certain, because man is self-evolutive. This is not to say that our evolution is entirely a matter of what we do. No less than in previous stages of God's creation, we also advance by pressures from outside us and by the work of the Holy Spirit within us. But still we have a responsibility, and the future is up to us in that we can either promote or thwart the work God is making. We are free to react either positively or negatively to the pressures to which we are subjected, and so move towards either greater or less personality. We are free to co-operate with or to resist the Holy Spirit within us, to move towards a closer union with God and the rest of mankind, or to move away from God and mankind.

This may be explained better if we turn again to the idea of giving up oneself, self-surrender, in traditional terms, sacrifice.[1] To be sure, it is our duty to press on and try to achieve something of value in the world, to work for positive and constructive results. But we must also give ourselves, be able to surrender our self-sufficiency, for the sake of entering into union with others, if our positive work is to be of much value. I must stress again that this self-giving does not mean the end of the self, but on the contrary its fulfilment.[2] In a union of love, those who unite do not become less themselves but more. It is the refusal to give oneself that leads to destruction and loss.

Self-giving is the pattern, not only of human action but of the whole of creation from the beginning, for it is necessary to any true union. As we have seen, the revelation of God's Triune nature shows us the same pattern even in him, Father, Son and Holy Ghost each giving himself completely to the others in a union which does not diminish distinction or confuse the Persons, but increases it so that they are both totally identified and totally differentiated. Then, as has been suggested, the beginning of creation must be understood as another act of self-giving, God as Trinity giving up his lack of limitations and posing over against himself a 'nothingness' from which he might create.

Now we must recognise that for creation to be complete God must elicit from it a response similar to his own action, a response which in the end must be a free response. The history of evolution shows us the different stages in the development of creation's response to God. From the beginning of creation from the Multiple, even the smallest elements have to give up their own sufficiency for the sake of a larger union which both identifies them with each other and makes them more truly themselves. Throughout evolution,

[1] Cf. A. D. Duncan, *The Whole Christ* (S.P.C.K., 1968), p. 16: 'The ultimate language is the language of sacrifice. Sacrifice is, if we could but grasp it, the principle upon which the whole of existence depends.'
[2] See *Le Milieu Divin*, Part II; 'My Universe', in *Science and Christ*, pp. 70–73; 'The Priest', in *Writings in Time of War*, p. 213.

from matter to life to man, the pattern remains the same. At each new stage a response of self-giving is called for from the elements which are to enter into the new union. So also human evolution brings about further advance, as a result of union, until the point is reached at which the final stage of creation can begin and creation give back to God a response similar to his own self-giving. God has, of course, been in his creation from the beginning, for it has taken the whole development of evolution to bring about the Incarnation:

> 'The first act of the Incarnation, the first appearance of the Cross, is marked by the plunging of the divine Unity into the ultimate depths of the Multiple. Nothing can enter into the universe that does not emerge from it. Nothing can be absorbed into things except through the road of matter, by ascent from plurality.'[1]

Yet for the actual appearance of Jesus, something more than God's unity with his material creation was required. From the material creation had to emerge mankind, and within mankind one who was capable of the complete love and obedience that God required. As Teilhard puts it:

> 'When the time had come when God resolved to realise his incarnation before our eyes, he had first of all to raise up in the world a virtue capable of drawing him as far as ourselves. He needed a mother who would engender him in the human sphere. What did he do? He created the Virgin Mary, that is to say he called forth on earth a purity so great that, within this transparency, he could concentrate himself to the point of appearing as a child.'[2]

Creation begins in God's self-giving which sets up the Multiple. The final act of creation begins with the self-giving of Mary to become 'the handmaid of the Lord', and the self-giving of God in which he 'concentrates himself to the

[1] 'My Universe', in *Science and Christ*, p. 60.
[2] *Le Milieu Divin* (Collins, Fontana Books, 1964), p. 134.

point of appearing as a child', entering into the creation as part of it, becoming incarnate and dying. In his perfect self-offering on the cross, Jesus 'recapitulates' not only the whole history of the self-giving of creation but also the inner life of God himself, uniting the two by the self-giving of both in a new creative union. Into this union, to bring creation to its completion, we must all enter, but enter freely.

If the pattern of the universe is really like this, then we may have a better idea of how creation is a means whereby God shows himself, and we may also know that human action is an integral part of evolution, bound up with the overall plan of creation and with the very life of God. We may also see something more of the nature of good and evil, and how human action can further God's work or, as sin, hinder it.

If the whole of creation is to some extent an image of the Trinity, this must be true above all of humanity. How do we have a Trinitarian nature, and is it as individuals or collectively that we may be found to have a trace of the Triune nature of God? The question is one which needs a great deal more study. We might possibly suggest that our three-fold nature is that we are matter, spirit and the capacity for further union, which involves both the individual and the social aspects of man. In any event, however, the image of the Trinity ought to be distinguished in us, the chief thing we know about the Trinity is the pattern of self-giving in union. Because we have a considerable measure of freedom, or, as Teilhard says, because we have become self-evolving, we are able to move towards union with God or to separate ourselves from God. Above all, we can refuse to let our lives be patterned on the model of the Trinity and the whole of creation by refusing to give ourselves to others and to God, by refusing to love, by closing in on our own self-sufficiency. In this way we are capable of frustrating the plan of the universe to the extent that we are involved in it as elements of the universe. We can follow the example of the Blessed Virgin Mary and let God work as he wills in us, we can allow Jesus to bring us into his own perfect union with the Father, or we can shut ourselves up in our own individuality and refuse to love. If we choose the latter option, we are also refusing to *be*, because our own continued being depends on our willingness to give up ourselves. Creative union always involves a sort of voluntary death, a giving up of oneself in love to find more being. A refusal to take part in the mutual self-giving which is the pattern alike of the creation of the universe and the life of God is the basic form of evil in man. Because union on the human level and higher can only be brought about through love, our response cannot be forced, and so we may either hasten or delay God's creative activity.

But the good is so much greater than the evil! If we can hinder God's purposes we can also further them. We have the capacity, since we are made in the image of the Trinity, to mirror the life of the Trinity not only in our individual lives but together as society, and to advance in union which both identifies and differentiates until we reach the Omega point of evolution, that is, until our union with Christ, which is also a union that differentiates, is complete. To put this another way, the pattern of the universe is self-giving. Our part is like that of Mary, to give ourselves to God so that Christ can be born through us, in the sense that the whole world is now being built and transformed into the Body of Christ by God's creative action working through the action of mankind united with and in Christ.

We must ask one further question: does creation add something to God, or does it ultimately have no effect at all on his complete self-sufficiency? I suggest that the answer is clear. Creation is an expression of God's perfection, his perfect union, not the determination of it. Creation in no way makes God, or is necessary for his perfection. Yet by the act of love with which he creates, God limits his self-sufficiency by making something which is not himself, so that his love gives an immense value to what he makes and he produces something which, as Teilhard says, he could have by no other means. We must hold two truths together:

3

God is entirely self-sufficient; and yet the universe brings him *something vitally necessary*.[1]

Teilhard pictures the entire realm of personal beings, the noosphere, completely united as one personal centre and detached from its material basis, becoming 'super-centred' in God. Just as within the Trinity the self-giving of the Persons does not lead to their confusion, so God's self-giving in creation neither diminishes him nor makes God any less himself. Similarly, in coming finally to perfect union with God, the universe will not become confused with God but will also be supremely itself while mirroring and sharing in the perfection of God's own union. In terms of the pattern we have been investigating, the final outcome of creation must surely be seen as the completion of the act with which it began. God limits himself in love, gives himself, to bring creation to birth. The Blessed Trinity extends the pattern of God's own life beyond himself to produce a creation through union and to give himself to us. May we not say then that the final sense of creation must be the completion of this movement by a perfect response from creation? That is, creation is complete when, through human action in Christ, it is brought to the point where it answers God's love by giving itself back to him, as a whole, a perfect image of God's own Triune being.

[1] *Christianisme et Évolution* (unpublished). My translation.

FOUR

The Place of Evil in a World of Evolution

R. B. SMITH

The problems posed by the fact of evil in the world are among the most baffling of any which face mankind. There is nothing new in man's wrestling, on both the intellectual and the practical levels, with sin, suffering, death. Is it possible, then, that the new perspectives opened up by modern science, 'advances' which seem at times to magnify the forces of evil, could provide a new hope for the solution of the age-old problems? Teilhard de Chardin claimed that the discovery of evolution, in particular, provides fresh evidence to explain the place of evil in the world and also indicates an approach whereby evil may be overcome. Although his writings are concerned chiefly with the positive side of evolution, he speaks also of 'the very great importance that the explicit consideration of evil is assuming in my thought.'[1] Let us try now to understand, in the light of Teilhard's writings, what the place of evil may be, remembering that the universe is an evolutionary process and, speaking theologically, interpreting God's creative act as a creating by means of evolution.

Immediately we face the difficulty that there is no systematic treatment of the problem of evil anywhere in Teilhard's writings, published or unpublished. In December 1917,

[1] Quoted by Claude Cuénot, *Teilhard de Chardin* (Burns & Oates, 1965), p. 396.

Teilhard noted in his diary that he was planning a study that would cover all the major aspects of evil.[1] Unfortunately, it would seem that this study never materialised. Teilhard did produce several short, tentative articles about different aspects of evil during the first world war, and several more on original sin in the early 1920s, up to the time of his banishment to China which was occasioned by one of these papers. After that virtually nothing on the subject appeared until the late 1940s. However, although he never explored evil systematically as a whole, Teilhard says enough about it in some of his writings and implies enough in others – e.g. in *The Phenomenon of Man*, where, as he says, it 'seeps out through every nook and cranny, every joint and sinew'[2] – that it is possible to construct a fairly detailed and systematic account of the place of evil, seen in the light of his thought.

There is a second difficulty. Some critics object that Teilhard has no doctrine of evil, and a few go so far as to deny that he was willing to recognise evil and imply that his vision of the world is an over-optimistic caricature of reality.[3] Others, more sympathetic, nevertheless suggest that Teilhard did not give sufficient consideration to the place of evil and to Christ's victory over evil on the cross.[4] On the other hand, Henri de Lubac insists that Teilhard's insights into the nature of evil are of very great value.[5] We must admit that Teilhard provides evidence to support either position. He spoke of blindness to evil as a 'mortal flaw',[6] and mentioned the fact that evil increases with the advance of evolution, so that 'the more man becomes man, the more the question of evil adheres and aggravates, in his flesh, in

[1] Quoted by Bruno de Solages, *Teilhard de Chardin* (Toulouse: Privat, 1967), p. 227 n.

[2] P. 309.

[3] See especially J.-M. Domenach, 'La personnalisme de Teilhard de Chardin', *Esprit* XXXI (1963), 353.

[4] See O. A. Rabut, *Dialogue with Teilhard de Chardin* (Sheed & Ward, 1961), p. 247; C. F. Mooney, *Teilhard de Chardin and the Mystery of Christ* (Collins, 1966), pp. 133, 142–144.

[5] *The Religion of Teilhard de Chardin* (Collins, 1967), Chapter 4.

[6] Quoted by Cuénot, *loc. cit.*

his nerves, in his spirit.'[1] But then in other passages he gives the impression of being a naïve optimist:

As a result of deeply rooted habits, the problem of evil continues automatically to be called insoluble. We must really ask why. . . . In our modern perspectives of a universe in the state of cosmogenesis, how is it that so many intelligent people obstinately refuse to see that, intellectually speaking, the famous problem *no longer exists*?[2]

In addition to examining these two approaches to the problem of evil, the one stressing its great importance and the other claiming that it is a non-existent problem, there are two other attitudes towards evil which we must investigate. The first is concerned with the difficulty of maintaining our belief in God's goodness in the face of the undoubted fact of evil. Teilhard maintains that evil is an inevitable accompaniment to creation, and adds that 'God seems to have been unable to create without entering into a struggle against evil'.[3] Evil is not the will of God, but something he will ultimately overcome. Yet in spite of his love, God cannot simply do away with evil at this stage of evolution: 'God *cannot*, now and at a single stroke, heal us and show himself'.[4] This is not because of any defect in God's power or goodness or in his love for us and concern for our well-being, but because of the nature of the creation itself.

The last attitude towards evil which we have to examine is exemplified by a passage in 'The Mystical Milieu', in which Teilhard seems to welcome evil, at least in some of its forms, and hail it as a friend. While it remains evil and must be resisted, evil can nevertheless be used by God to bring us into closer union with him:

'Blessed then be the disappointments which snatch the cup from our lips; blessed be the chains which force us to go

[1] 'L'Energie spirituelle de la Souffrance', in *L'Activation de l'Energie* (Paris: Seuil, 1963), p. 225. My translation.

[2] *Comment je vois* (unpublished). My translation.

[3] 'My Universe', in *Science and Christ* (Collins, 1968), p. 80.

[4] *Comment je crois* (unpublished). My translation.

where we would not. Blessed be relentless time and the unending thraldom in which it holds us. . . . Blessed, above all, be death and the horror of falling back into the cosmic forces.'[1]

These four very different attitudes to evil all form part of the system of Teilhard de Chardin, and we cannot safely ignore any of them without running the risk of destroying something valuable in his thought. They appear contradictory, but in fact they must all be understood in their relation to the central and unifying concept of evolution. I propose to show how in the light of evolution they may be regarded as complementary, and how they all illustrate different but true aspects of the very complex question of evil.

Belief that the universe is developing through a convergent evolution is a unifying thread running through all Teilhard's writings. Just as it provides the suggestion from which he developed not only his scientific theories but his philosophical and theological ones as well, so it also gives a clue to be followed in all discussions of evil. Evolution makes a great difference. If the universe is a fixed system or if it is something that moves in a cyclical fashion without any real progress, then evil is something which is inexplicably 'there', and a search for its place or origin is a hopeless task. However, in the perspective of evolution it is now possible even on a purely natural level, leaving out theology for the time being, to trace the development of evil and to see what function it has in the world process. While it is doubtless an exaggeration to say that in a perspective of cosmogenesis the problem of evil 'ne se pose plus',[2] this perspective may well point the way to a solution to the problem. In spite of his sometimes over-optimistic utterances, evil remained a mystery to Teilhard, as it must always remain a mystery. Evolution, however, contributes to the solution of the problem by giving us a vastly increased insight into the nature of the mystery.

If we examine evil as a phenomenon, it seems to bear a definite relationship to the advance of evolution. In *The*

---

[1] *Writings in Time of War* (Collins, 1968), p. 131 f.
[2] 'Du Cosmos à la Cosmogénèse', in *L'Activation de l'Energie*, p. 267.

Phenomenon of Man and various other writings, Teilhard describes a law of recurrence, which he names the Law of Complexity and Consciousness. According to this, evolution progresses along a definite axis of ascent, towards ever-increasing organic complexity and inward spontaneity or consciousness, which vary in direct proportion to each other. It almost seems that evil is so closely related to the advance of evolution that it might also be included in the formula, as varying in direct proportion to complexity and consciousness. However, this is only an appearance. Evil, as a force of disintegration, cannot conceivably continue to increase indefinitely into the future and reach the Omega point together with personal being. By its very nature as destructive, it must ultimately either disappear, overcome by good, or triumph over good, in which case its increase will bring about the decrease of complexity and consciousness. In either event, the relationship must cease to be one of direct proportion.[1] But we must add that while it would be a gross over-simplification to hold that complexity, consciousness, and evil vary in direct ratio to one another, there must none the less be some connection, for it is a fact that there is both a greater quantity of evil and a more serious quality of evil to be found at the higher stages of evolution than at the lower ones. In particular, human evil, that is, evil at the highest point evolution has so far reached, is a far more serious matter than pre-human evil.

'By the very fact of its appearance,' Teilhard writes, 'thought is an element of disintegration, of decomposition, for the living stem.'[2] Perhaps this is so, but does it mean that there is *necessarily* a greater evil where there is thought than where there is not thought? The answer must be that it is not necessarily so, for if man is distinguished by his capacity for self-guided evolution, made possible by reflective

---

[1] Cf. Dorothy Emmet, *Whitehead's Philosophy of Organism* (Macmillan, 1966), p. 269: 'While evil is positive, it is also destructive, and in the end self-destructive.'

[2] Letter of 1 January 1917, *The Making of a Mind* (Collins, 1965), p. 160.

thought, then human self-evolution might conceivably have moved in a direction that would lead to the diminishment of evil. In reality, of course, there has been a tremendous increase in both the quantity and the quality. Now, because evil does appear in an especially acute form at the highest point of evolution, it is here that it must be defined. Seeing man in the context of evolution, Teilhard defines the 'good' as that which tends towards the increase of complexity and consciousness, or, in different terms, that which tends towards further development of the personal, in both its individual and its collective forms. Similarly, we may now define evil as movement which opposes or limits the growth of complexity and consciousness or the personal. But just as consciousness itself appears clearly for the first time in man, and as it is only in the light of human consciousness that an 'inward' aspect is attributed to the rest of creation, so also evil appears clearly for the first time in man, and the disorders and pain on the lower levels of evolution are said to be evil only because they are part of the process that leads to human evil.

Treating evil as a part of the total phenomenon of man in the universe, we may distinguish three basic types of evil, each characteristic of one of the major 'zones' of evolution:[1]

(a) There is a form of evil which is a tendency towards disorder and disunion, found throughout the universe along with a tendency towards order and union. In the zone of the pre-living this is the only kind of evil discernible. At that stage also, the question of its 'evilness' may be disputed; it appears as a necessary condition for advance, and a small enough price for the success of so valuable a project as evolution. On the human level, however, it appears clearly as an evil. It is not only a small portion of humanity that must advance, as happened with material particles, but humanity as a whole. Evolution can no longer afford wastage

---

[1] Teilhard outlines the following three points in 'L'Evolution de la Responsibilité dans le Monde', in *L'Activation de l'Energie*, p. 215. A different classification of evil under four headings is given in *The Phenomenon of Man* (Collins, 1959), p. 310.

or drop-outs. Mankind is converging on itself, being welded into one personal unit, and therefore any advance must be the advance of the whole, for we can no longer tolerate the idea of a portion of humanity failing to evolve any farther or another part falling back to a lower level. We are part of each other, and what affects one affects all.

(b) There is the evil of suffering and pain, in which man is one with all living creatures. Like disintegration, this kind of evil is in its origin related to progress, and therefore its appearance in the world seems quite natural. Reproduction and *death* are a means of advance primarily, and suffering is associated largely with the death. In man, however, pain has become not so much a spur to advance as a dissuasive against it, because we are able to foresee further suffering as a result of our efforts to advance. Teilhard's main concern was to show how suffering may be transformed and used constructively, by offering it to God for the advance of the world, to bring out to a greater extent the 'within', the spiritual.

(c) Moral evil is the specifically human form of evil. Its effects are seen in nature but it originates in man. The possibility of moral evil follows from the fact of human freedom or self-evolution. It appears as a turning aside from the true line of advance. This is not necessarily a guilty opposition to evolution, because it is very often the result of a necessary experiment which goes in the wrong direction, a consequence of ignorance or of groping for the right way and failing to find it. Other times, it can only be attributed to sheer perversity. There is no question about the evil nature of this. It is obviously evil, and it must be overcome.

Looking at evil in the perspective of evolution we may now be able to see the pattern of its development. It originates from the disunity at the base of evolution, and in its most elementary form is simply the tendency of the products of evolution to decompose or to develop in directions that preclude further advance. There is no particular problem left here. Disorder and the tendency to disunity are clearly part of the material basis on which evolution is built, and evil extends from there throughout creation. Pain and suffering are a transformation of this elementary form of evil at a higher stage of being. In itself, suffering is often an incentive to progress, even though it results in part from progress. Even moral evil, understood as primarily a groping towards further evolutionary advance, either of the individual or of mankind as a whole, has quite a reasonable place in a world which is in evolution.

However, we must never forget that Teilhard's analysis of evolution shows that something beyond evolution is necessary for its continuation and stability. While it is not legitimate to conclude that science, or a philosophy based on science, requires belief in God, Teilhard maintains that a synthesis of scientific belief in evolution and the Christian doctrine of God leads to new strength and new insights for both, and therefore he accepts and integrates into his system not only a phenomenology but also a full Christian belief. Now the question of evil reappears, but it is a slightly different question this time. Christian faith is not content to accept the fact that evil may have an easily explained place in evolution. It demands why this is so – how is it that there can be evil in God's creation if God is both loving and all-powerful? This is an old question for Christians, both as a practical problem in our own lives and as a theoretical one when non-Christians point to the undoubted fact of evil as an argument against God. However, it is a question which must be raised again, because the synthesis between Christian faith and scientific belief in evolution provides new and valuable suggestions as to an answer.

I must make it clear at this point that when we considered evil as part of the phenomenon of man we first accepted the fact that there is such a thing as evolution and that it does have a definite direction of movement. Then, with this belief in the background, we examined evil. Similarly, when we come now to see the relationship between God and evil we must begin with acceptance of the positive side, the Christian faith, and consider evil in the light of our faith. This means that we must accept the fact, from a Christian and evolutionary point of view, that God is creating the world by means of evolution – Teilhard calls it 'création évolutive' – and that this creation is moving from a state of nothingness, characterised by complete dissociation, towards complete personal union with God in Jesus Christ. If we start here it may be possible to understand something of the 'why' of evil. If we begin with evil, we can never possibly hope to arrive at a positive conclusion of any value, but if we first accept the positive side, we can with profit examine the negative and come to a better understanding of the place of evil in God's creation.

We must see evil especially in its relation to the method of creation and the goal of creation. If creation were a once-for-all act of God in bringing into existence a completed work, then evil would be totally inexplicable. It might perhaps be regarded as the result of divine caprice, or alternatively as due entirely to sinful man. On the other hand, contemporary knowledge of evolution suggests that this is not at all a correct picture of creation, and so a fresh examination is needed. Creation is not an instantaneous bringing into existence of a finished work. In fact, creation is not finished but is still going on.

Combining his knowledge of evolution and its direction with his Christian belief, Teilhard de Chardin proposes on the theological and philosophical level of his thought a theory of 'creative union' or 'evolutive creation'. That is, creation is itself an action whereby God brings things into existence through a process of union which we call evolution. It is important to note that Teilhard does not say that evolution itself is creative, but that creation is evolutive. Creation is definitely the work of God, not of any forces inherent in the natural process itself. Creation is a process – 'evolutive' – but God brings about real novelty or 'creation' at the level of each new union. Where there is no union at all there is nothing. Through union God brings his creation into being. Through the continuing process of evolution, God is bringing his creation to ever higher states of being.

The doctrine of the Trinity is very important here. God has revealed himself as Three in One, which is to say that he himself is not a static unity but a dynamic union of three. God IS because he is perfect union.[1] If God in his own nature were not Triune but a numerical unity, there would be no creation. Because God himself exists in uniting himself, he brings his creation into existence by a gradual process of union, drawing it forwards to complete union with himself.

Hence the traditional notion of 'being' as a self-evident and ultimate concept must be abandoned. Contrary to the idea that 'being' is a common-sense concept which cannot be reduced to anything more basic, we must affirm that evolution shows being itself to be founded on a dynamic movement, that of union. Accordingly, Teilhard gives two formulas:

'to be = to unite oneself or to unite others;
to be = to be united and unified by another.'[2]

This idea of being as a result of union is based on contemporary knowledge of evolution, reinforced by the doctrine of the Holy Trinity.

Now, God who exists in uniting must, if he is God, be entirely self-sufficient. However, God's revelation to man, and in particular the Incarnation of his Son, shows the immense value he places on his creation. We must conclude that in some way, not from necessity but because he so wills it, God achieves himself by creating, even though his creative act springs from his self-sufficient perfection. Teilhard borrows one of St Paul's phrases to express the mystery, and says that in creating God is building up the fullness of his Christ, that he is making something which is to be taken up into personal union with his own nature, through the Second Person of the Trinity who is himself the synthesis between the divine Creator and his creation.[3]

If this is true, then creation could only be by one means,

---

[1] *Introduction à la vie chrétienne* (unpublished): 'God himself, in a rigorously true sense, does not exist, *save in uniting himself.*' (My translation).

[2] *Comment je vois.* See also 'La Centrologie', in *L'Activation de l'Energie*, p. 120.

[3] 'My Universe', in *Science and Christ*, p. 79.

a gradual unification, little by little, under God's attractive influence, using as a means of advance the play of large numbers and natural selection under pressure at the lower levels of evolution, and using in addition to these at the higher levels the free and spontaneous co-operation of personal beings. The development of 'persons' for personal union with him could not be achieved by the exercise of force but only by divine love. Therefore God does not intervene directly to interrupt the process of his creation, but rather he directs it by the force of his attraction from ahead and by the working of the incarnate Christ, Omega already present within evolution, as well as by the influence of the Holy Spirit indwelling every part of creation. In such a process, where God does not directly compel but urges and where he depends on the reactions of his creatures for the furtherance of their creation, then, as Teilhard says, 'evil appears necessarily and as abundantly as you like in the course of evolution – not by accident (which would not much matter) but through the very structure of the system'.[1]

We see, then, that even when Christianity and evolution come together, that is, when the theological element is added to our picture of the world, evolution provides the clue which makes it possible to believe in God in spite of the fact of evil. God is responsible for evil in that it follows from the fact that he creates, but at the same time the presence of evil does not contradict Christian belief in God's love and sovereignty.

Surely, though, it will be objected, God might have made a creation which did not include evil as a side-effect? Possibly indeed, for who can say what is possible with God? However, Teilhard rightly refused to consider the question. There is no point at all in speculating about hypothetical possible worlds; *this* world is the one we are concerned with. God could only create a world which is evolving towards a free union of persons with him in the way he did create it. Therefore we must maintain that evil is to some extent unavoidable as a side-effect of a process leading to the personal.

[1] *The Phenomenon of Man*, p. 311.

Up to this point we have been considering evil in general, rather than specifically human evil. Now we must turn to what has traditionally been regarded as the origin of human evil, the fall of man and that vexing question of 'original sin'.

Teilhard takes the Biblical view that it is the *whole* of creation that will be redeemed by Christ, that the final salvation of man will include the salvation and transfiguration of the universe of which man is a part. Therefore, says Teilhard, to have a part in salvation the universe as a whole must first have been involved in evil. Whether or not this follows, we have seen that evil is to be found throughout the universe. In order to explain why the whole universe needs salvation, Teilhard understands original sin to mean 'the essential reaction of the finite to the creative act.'[1] That is to say, because creation is not yet finished it always has a tendency to resist God and to move backwards towards lower states of union. Putting it in pictorial form, Teilhard suggests that creation may be envisaged as a pyramid. At the bottom it continues down indefinitely to an ever-widening base. At the top it reaches the Omega point. In this picture, original sin is represented by the complete disunion of the base of the pyramid, with its tendency to drag the entire structure down to disorder and disunion. At each level of progress there is a 'fall', which is simply the realisation of some of the tendencies to move backwards or to fail to advance. The Fall of man is more serious than any pre-human fall simply because men are higher creatures and have a greater distance from which to fall.

The chief merit of this theory is that it provides a unified account of the origin of all evil. It also stresses a fact which Christians long tended to deny, that evil in many of its forms, including death, existed on earth long before the coming of man and therefore could not possibly be the result of man's sin.

However, there are four major difficulties involved in this same explanation:

(*a*) The personal element is not clear. In what way are

[1] *Chute, Rédemption et Géocentrie* (unpublished). My translation.

we responsible for human evil? The Christian teaching is that man is responsible for his sin, but this theory might imply a denial of our responsibility for evil.

(b) The traditional doctrine of original sin describes sin as the *cause* of disorder and the tendency to turn from God. Teilhard reverses this and sees sin as the *effect* of disorder. Is the change legitimate?

(c) The responsibility for evil is placed squarely on God and his method of creation. Here again we must ask whether man does not in fact bear some of the guilt?

(d) As Teilhard himself admits, there seems to be 'an excess of evil' in the world, above and beyond what can readily be explained as a normal effect of evolution.

In traditional belief, man's responsibility is clearly maintained, and God's goodness upheld. The difficulties of the traditional view of original sin, and in particular the difficulties of acceptance of Genesis 3 as literally true, are primarily that there is no real connection made between evil in man and evil in the rest of the world, and that no account is taken of any evil that existed before man appeared in evolution.

Both sets of difficulties may be overcome, I suggest, and the strength of both positions preserved, if instead of accepting either the traditional view of sin or Teilhard's explanation, we take the two together and attempt to form a synthesis. There is indeed, we must admit, an evil which originates in man, something more serious than what we have described from a phenomenological point of view as 'moral evil'. There is something that begins with man, for only this can account for the 'excess of evil' that exists in the world, an actual opposition to God and his purposes – sin. Yet undoubtedly there is also evil which did not originate with mankind, although clearly it affects man. This latter type of evil, which Teilhard mistakenly calls 'original sin', may well, I suggest, be the *occasion* of the Fall of man and the coming of real original sin. The account in the third chapter of Genesis could easily be interpreted in this way, for the serpent which tempted Eve is a representative of nature, evolution before man with its limitations and its tendencies to disorder and regression. Natural evil is not the direct cause of sin, but it may provide a temptation to sin. The actual turning against God which is sin, however mysterious its origin and transmission, could only be a free act of mankind. Once man has sinned, however, the effects of the rebellion spread beyond man to affect pre-human evolution. Thus sin increases natural evil, which in turn provides an increased temptation to sin, and so on.

While this sketch is obviously an oversimplification and leaves many unresolved problems, nevertheless some such combination of theories may serve as a corrective to Teilhard's position. His concept of original disorder as the source of evil is a fruitful one, but it needs to be balanced by the traditional belief that man is a major source of evil. The combination has the advantage of meeting most of the difficulties of each theory taken separately. It keeps the connection between man and the evolutionary process that produced him. At the same time it gives an explanation of the 'excess of evil' which cannot be explained as a purely natural consequence of evolution. It preserves the element of personal responsibility for sin, rather than denying even by implication either the love or the power of God. There is a proper and necessary place in an evolutionary outlook for belief in original sin, but only when it is combined with another account of evil such as that which Teilhard gives.

But still we must ask why God permits evil. Without the knowledge of evolution the only answer we could really suggest is that all evil results from human sin. But evolution has shown that this is simply not true: suffering and death were in the world long before man. There is another possible answer: God is preparing through his evolutive creation something of great value which could not be had any other way. Therefore natural evil is, at least to some extent, a necessary consequence of his purposes. Sin, which helps also explain the excess of natural evil, is not a necessary by-product of evolution except in the secondary sense that the possibility of sin is a necessity. An evolutive creation must include disorder and a tendency to regression, and involves also the probability of animal suffering and the possibility of human sin with all its consequences. God cannot stop it short without stopping his act of creation. However, evolution also suggests, as Christian belief affirms, that God will not tolerate evil ultimately but that he is in fact working to bring it to an end. In Christ, he is working within his creation to overcome evil. When creation is complete, evil will have been completely overcome.

There is a traditional dilemma concerning God and evil, and most attempts to come to grips with the problem have been caught on one horn or the other.[1] The positions are probably best represented by St Thomas Aquinas on the one hand and the German philosopher Leibniz on the other. Aquinas, anxious to maintain the sovereignty of God, claimed that God could indeed have created a better world than this, but that he could not better have made this world and it is not capable of being improved. Now if we accept this argument we indeed affirm the omnipotence of God, but we are involved in the suggestion that his love and goodness are not all they might be. Leibniz, on the other hand, anxious at all costs to maintain the love of God, taught that this is the best of all possible worlds. If we accept this, we are implying that God is not omnipotent.

Evolution enables us to escape from the dilemma by showing that there is one mistake common to both positions. There is some truth to both, but both are wrong because they have as an unexpressed premise the belief that creation is a completed act. Since we now know that creation is not finished, we can break down the dilemma and affirm with confidence both the love and the power of God. Aquinas was right in saying that God could make a better world than this, but he was wrong in believing that this world cannot be improved, because it is *this* world that God destines to become the best possible world when it reaches its perfection in him. God can make a better creation than this, but at the same

[1] See John Hick, *Evil and the God of Love* (Macmillan, 1966), pp. 100, 170.

time this is the best of all possible worlds because it is this world that God is leading to a perfect consummation.

We have now considered how it is that, seen in one of its aspects, 'the famous problem [i.e. the problem of evil] no longer exists', while at the same time we must recognise that as a practical problem, 'the more man becomes man, the more the question of evil adheres and aggravates, in his flesh, in his nerves, in his spirit.' We have seen also what Teilhard means when he says that 'God seems to have been unable to create without entering into a struggle against evil', and that it is not due to any failure in God's love or goodness, but rather to the limitations of the present state of creation, that God cannot immediately overcome all evil and bring us to perfection.

There yet remains to be considered the last of the quotations with which I began, and the attitude towards evil which it typifies:

'Blessed then be the disappointments which snatch the cup from our lips; blessed be the chains which force us to go where we would not. Blessed be relentless time and the unending thraldom in which it holds us. . . . Blessed, above all, be death and the horror of falling back into the cosmic forces.'

Obviously there must be more to an analysis of evil than simply an examination of the form it takes in evolution and of the reasons why God permits it to continue. Teilhard holds also that evil exercises a positive role, that, while it is a force of opposition to God, God is able to take and use it for his purposes. Therefore, in a way, it must be welcomed. This is not to say that evil is not evil: it is, and as such it must always be resisted. But because evil may be overcome, and because God uses it to bring about good, there is also a 'bright side' to it. To find this bright side we must see what God does about evil and what we must do about it.

Human action in overcoming evil is immensely important. We cannot leave the future entirely to God because his plan for us includes our co-operation in our own future. Omega does not force evolution to advance beyond the human stage, but draws it on by attraction from ahead: God does not compel us to come to him, but his love draws us. We may either co-operate or rebel. We must co-operate in order to bring creation to a successful outcome.[1]

Teilhard suggests several ways in which we may co-operate with God to advance creation. We must, to begin with, remain 'open' to each other, because any true advance of man must be the advance of mankind as a whole. Therefore we ought not to shut ourselves up in our own little individualities but open ourselves to others. Second, mankind must press on with the development of the 'Within', that is, we must seek by research to extend our knowledge in all areas of life, so that human consciousness and personality may continue to develop and expand. We need not be afraid that the advances of science will mean the loss of our personality. There is always the danger that any form of pressure will lead to our reacting in the wrong way, but so long as we remain 'open' to each other and to further evolutionary development, scientific advance can only serve to enhance personal values, for it is in the same line of evolution as that which produced personality. At the same time, however, in order for our personal centres to become joined in a total personal union of love with each other and supercentred in Omega – speaking theologically, for us to become fully united with each other and with God in Christ – we must in some way be 'broken open' so that God's love may take possession of us. If it were not for sin, this might happen as a natural development. As it is, while such a natural development may still come about in the future, and Teilhard gives good reasons for believing it may, at the present time God brings about good through evil. In death we lose our individuality, surrendering it to God, but in it also God takes our personality and preserves us eternally as persons in union with himself.

Teilhard sees the present conditions of the world, the over-crowding, the pressures on mankind for more complex and

[1] Letter of 12 July 1918, *The Making of a Mind*, p. 214.

more efficient organisation, as being necessary in order to force us to respond and advance.[1] In view of the pressures bearing in on man with increasing force, we must make some response. In this response lies the advance of evolution, if we respond in the direction of ever-increasing knowledge and consciousness and of love for one another, instead of rebelling and forcing a reversal. Ahead of us lies another 'critical point' of evolution, at which our personalities must become joined centre-to-centre in a true union of persons in love. By forcing us to make some response, evil in any form may be used by God as a means to make us advance, and as such it is his instrument and may be called blessed.

What now is the final end of humanity? One of the major aims of Teilhard's writings is to assure men that evil cannot finally triumph. If the universe were such that man was headed towards total death, then the universe would be revealed as senseless and as incapable of producing the sort of creatures it has produced. We must maintain that in order for man to function in a self-evolutionary manner, which he is doing at the present time, there must be ahead of men an Omega, the 'Prime Mover ahead', whose function it is to bring evolution to its completion, which lies in the direction of more personality, not less, of good, not evil. Finally, Teilhard writes, we come to escape from evil of all kinds through joining in a centre-to-centre union with Omega, which may come as a detachment from the womb of matter and may have the appearance of death, but is actually death and resurrection, 'the *hominisation* of death itself'.[2]

Christianity provides a final assurance for human action. The death and resurrection of Christ are evidence that God can overcome evil and that he has acted to overcome it. In the work of Christ on the Cross, suffering and evil must be continued unceasingly in the direction of increasing complexity/consciousness; human personality must press on towards its completion and totalisation in Christ. In

[1] See the letter of 1 September 1926, *Letters from a Traveller* (Collins, 1962), p. 132.
[2] *The Phenomenon of Man*, p. 272.

God's acceptance and transformation of our efforts and ourselves, we shall find the final solution to the problem of evil.[1]

[1] *Christologie et Evolution* (unpublished). See also 'L'Energie spirituelle de la souffrance', in *L'Activation de l'Energie*, p. 256.

FIVE

Progress

H. A. BLAIR

There can be few tasks more futile than the attempt to assess an author critically without first understanding his use of terms. It may be said that we have all realised this so far as Père Teilhard de Chardin is concerned, and that this is why those of us who read him make it our first business to unravel the meaning of those terms in his books which at first sight leave us guessing. Complexification, hominisation, granulation, polymerisation and many others – not all of them inventions of his own – are terms which clearly call out to be looked at with care.

For that very reason there is little danger in these obscurities. At least we realise that they are obscurities. The real danger lies in an author's use of perfectly familiar terms which we suppose ourselves to understand, though in fact he is using them in one sense and we are reading them in another.

One such word is *progress*, which Père Teilhard uses in a very special sense and which, if only because of the known variety of its meanings, his critics should have taken care to read in the sense in which he used it. One or two passages from his letters, if they do not entirely make clear what he does mean, do at least make it quite clear what he does not.

In a letter to Max Bégouen[1] Teilhard is answering Bégouen's doubt whether success in a commercial enterprise can bring *moral* progress. He shows how it can do so:

[1] *Letters from a Traveller* (Fontana ed., 1967), pp. 119 f.

'I answer, "In this way, that since everything holds together in a world which is on the way to unification, the spiritual success of the universe is bound up with the correct functioning of every zone of that universe and particularly with the release of every possible energy in it. Because your understanding – which I take to be perfectly legitimate – is going well, a little more health is being spread in the human mass, and in consequence a little more liberty to act, to think and to love. Whatever we do, we can and we must do it with the strengthening and broadening consciousness of working, individually, to achieve a result which (even as a tangible reality) is required, at least indirectly, by the body of Christ. As you say yourself, to the value of the work done is added the value of the actual doing, which by its fidelity creates in us the personality expected of us by Christ." '

This justifies the euphoria which Bégouen has felt, and which he is uneasy at having felt.

'Because you are doing the best you can (even though you may sometimes fail), you are forming your own self within the world, and you are helping the world to form itself around you. How then could you fail from time to time to feel overcome by the boundless joy of creation?'

In another letter,[1] to Léontine Zanta, he writes:

'Now in the vast solitudes of Mongolia (which from the human point of view are a static and dead region), I see the same thing as I saw long ago at the "front" (which from the human point of view was the most alive thing that existed): one single operation is in process of happening in the world, and it alone can justify our action: the emergence of some spiritual reality, through and across the efforts of life.'

These passages should make clear something of his meaning when he uses the word *progress*.

One of the criticisms of him has been that, while progress

[1] *Letters to Léontine Zanta* (Collins, 1968), p. 52.

is fundamental to his frame of thought, there is no real evidence of progress in the sense of improvement. These critics assume that Teilhard's thesis looks back on history and pre-history, and sees there a gradual moral and spiritual advance. But is this true? It seems to me that it is not. What he does claim is that the potentiality for good increases as time unfolds. His phrase is 'increased power for increased action',[1] but he warns us that unless it is properly used it may be not creative but destructive:

> 'As things are now going it will not be long before we run full tilt into one another. . . . A new domain of psychical expansion – that is what we lack. And it is staring us in the face if we would only raise our heads to look at it.'[2]

Progress then means not a sort of Spencerian over-confidence in ourselves (an over-confidence which even in Spencer hardly out-lasted the first edition of the *First Principles*), nor a necessary claim that we are better than our fathers, but a recognition that our opportunities are greater, and therefore our responsibility more frightening: a thesis that few would care to deny. In this sense progress is fundamental to the theme of *The Phenomenon*. Man is acquiring more and more opportunities for seeing the universe as it is, and himself within that universe; and this is something which he can only do in one of two ways. Either he must think theoretically, by the use of logic and philosophy; or he must think historically and scientifically, by the use of evidence and experiment. But whichever way he thinks, his thought will be influenced and indeed perverted by his physical state of health, by his environment and by psychological forces beyond his control. These will affect historical and scientific thinking more drastically than logical and philosophic thinking. Therefore the nearer man approaches to pure thought (the noosphere) the more objective he can become: the more objective he can become the more he will free

[1] *Phenomenon of Man* (Collins, 6th impr., 1960), p. 251.
[2] *Ibid.*, p. 253.

himself from illusion, and particularly (Teilhard says) from the three great illusions.

I am reminded of the saying of Anaxagoras:

'Whereas all other things have in them a portion of everything, Mind is unlimited and self-ruled, and is not mixed with anything, but is just alone by itself.

'For if it were not by itself but were mixed with anything else, it would partake of all things, if it were mixed with any (for in everything there is a portion of everything, as I said before), and the things mixed with it would prevent it from having power over anything in the same way that it has being alone by itself. For it is the thinnest of all things and the purest, and it has all knowledge about everything and the greatest strength.

'And Mind has power over all things, greater and smaller, that have life.'[1]

Like other great thinkers, the originality of Teilhard consists not in saying things never said before, but in making the old things acceptable in a new age.

The first illusion of which man must rid himself is the physicist's illusion of smallness: that we are merely microbes on a comparatively insignificant planet in a middle-class solar system in a fairly commonplace galaxy: that we can make no claims to any sort of position of importance, let alone centrality, in the universe. But if what is distilled from the whole process is Mind, observable at last in humanity; and if this which has happened can, not unreasonably, be regarded as the purpose of, because the result of, the whole process – seen as a purpose now because of the element of purposefulness which is an undeniable quality of that same Mind which has emerged; and if there seems no reason to doubt that the brew which has distilled Mind is still brewing something beyond Mind as we now know it; then the smallness that the physicist is tempted to talk about is quite

[1] *Anaxagoras: fragment* 12. Translated in F. M. Cornford, *Greek Religious Thought* (Dent, 1923), pp. 124 f.

irrelevant. The brew which is being boiled up is there for the very purpose of the spirit which is distilled from it, and the rest can go back to the compost heap.

The second illusion is the mathematician's illusion of plurality, which Pythagoras resolved into the ultimate unity through the medium of music.

> 'From harmony, from heavenly harmony,
>   This universal frame began.
> From harmony to harmony
>   Through all the compass of the notes it ran,
>   The diapason closing full in man.'[1]

Though, of course, Teilhard could not go all the way with Dryden, since man for him was only a stage in the progress towards what he could do no more than name without knowing – point Omega.

Not that plurality is in every sense an illusion. As we probe our way back into the past, or speculate our way into the future, plurality is real, but only as a mental concept. Thought has to break things up and analyse them; yet, as Aristotle pointed out, the philosopher must realise that what he isolates and dockets in his mind is not really a separate entity. Elements and parts cannot be cut off in chunks from a system which, through polymerisation, is so much interwoven that it is indivisible.

It is therefore a totum, in which we find infinite similarity of pattern but never repetition. The stages from atomic to molecular, up to astronomical proportions, show not merely a difference in scale but also difference in structure, though the patterns are comparable. Macrocosm is not simply magnified microcosm. In this system the influence of each unit is 'co-extensive with the whole of space'.[2] Through the new thinking which has accompanied the quantum theory, the atom is no longer a very small bit of matter, or even a parcel of finite energy, but an 'infinitesimal centre of the world itself'.[3] So the whole universe is seen as interdependent

[1] J. Dryden, 'Song for St Cecilia's Day, 1687', in Palgrave's *Golden Treasury* (O.U.P., 1950), p. 49.
[2] *Phenomenon*, p. 45.　　[3] *Ibid.*, p. 46.

and in continual movement which must be measured in *duration*: that is, by a yardstick which is a purely intellectual concept (not successional) which we call space-time.

Plurality therefore is summed up and classified by Mind in the sort of unity which can reasonably be seen, not indeed as the end and aim of evolution, but as pointing towards, and providing an instrument for, the attainment of a final end named but indescribable.

Teilhard, however, will not have it that the unity behind plurality is simply a mental concept. He sees complexification beginning in a movement probably triggered off by an elemental

'explosion, pulverising a primitive quasi-atom within which space-time would be strangulated (in a sort of natural absolute zero) at only some milliards of years behind us'.[1]

But the tendency remained in the fragments to seek an unity only denied by the force of the original explosion: therefore while the universe expands in space-time (the only possible four-dimensional direction), the fragments re-unite in groups. This he describes as granulation, which he sees present as a tendency both in the 'without' and the 'within'.

Plurality is an illusion because the universe is dynamic and moving towards the unity of the totum. On this Teilhard's thesis certainly depends, but not on the idea of progress in any ordinary sense. There need not be improvement, but there can be – and there should be – and there will be, if men realise their responsibilities.

This they certainly will not do unless they break free from the third of the great illusions, the illusion of *immobility*. This is the illusion that events, institutions and processes can be stopped and stood up and looked at. It was a Greek philosophic school which coined the phrase πάντα ῥεῖ, all things are fluid: to the 'flowing philosophers' change was the only constant. Those who understand this will be, like Teilhard, free from the illusion that any static picture can be true – for instance, of Zeno's arrow in flight.

[1] *Phenomenon*, p. 47 n.

This is one of the fundamentals in Teilhard's system which makes no claim to novelty; in fact, very little that he says is new, but his genius lies in so co-ordinating a number of ideas already known in other times that they make sense for our time. This is after all true genius, and can be happily compared with the pathetic attempts of others to say things which have never been said before. Jesus Christ himself said little that had not been said before: his genius lay in making old things new, and Teilhard is his disciple.

Evolution shows a world in which nothing remains the same from one moment to another, and thought belongs to that world. The universe is dynamic without and within, and the two sides of it behave in the same sort of way. As we trace its progress we become (as nearly as we can) objective when we look at past history, because we can see it (or as much as we can see of it) as a whole. The trouble is that we can never see enough of it, and though we see what we do see objectively, our view is still unbalanced because of what we still cannot see. What we cannot see we have to guess at, and the guesses of the physicists do not agree with the guesses of the biologists, nor indeed those of the biologists and palaeontologists with each other. It is in the matter of these guesses that Teilhard is sharply criticised. What he calls 'the automatic suppression of the peduncles'[1] means that we can never find actual evidence of the growth of a new phylum. As far as we can see, first it is not there and then it is. This is well enough known as far as *homo sapiens* is concerned, but Teilhard points out that it is a rule which holds good throughout the whole process; and that is why our evidence is of the logical rather than the empirical kind as often as not. Looking at the whole picture as far as it is available to us, evolution is the most reasonable hypothesis; but it cannot be proved scientifically.

If it is accepted as a working hypothesis, as it surely must be, it means that the universe is in continual movement, not necessarily from less good to more good, but in a general direction. It need not be moving steadily in that direction:

[1] *Phenomenon*, p. 90.

it may be swinging from side to side like a pendulum, with or without any alteration in the length of swing. It may be following a spiral course: if so the result might look not unlike the seasons of the year, which follow a general similarity of pattern but are never twice the same. An alternative is a great cycle, at the end of which events repeat themselves exactly: this was the belief of the Jains and the Stoics, and certain sections of the Hindus and even Buddhists. These views form two general groups, the directional and the cyclic, possibly reflected in the two schools of thought in astro-physics – the 'big bang' theory and the 'continuous creation' theory.

The former is the one generally in favour at the moment, and it is the one which Teilhard accepts. It is interesting to see how consistent it is with his general thesis, and how inconsistent with some of the criticisms that have been made of him. An eminent Methodist remarked to me, 'I have read *The Phenomenon*, but I can see no sign in it of a Fall or of an Atonement'. I cannot remember what I then answered, but I would now say that he was not writing about the Fall, which was the primaeval explosion, and that he sees a gradual Atonement taking place in the whole process. There is some reason to believe that early in his career he accepted the doctrine of a pre-cosmic Fall, that the origin of evil lay in the spiritual sphere before creation, through which the material universe inherited a kind of twist or disorder, and that history tells of the restoration of a universe sadly out of joint. This is consistent with the thesis of *The Phenomenon*, which therefore becomes not the gradual emergence of an order which had never been before, but the restoration of an order which had been destroyed, in such a way as not to infringe the universal principle of free will. God behaves in the same way as Kingsley's Mother Carey, who does something more wonderful than making things: he makes things make themselves. This is the insight of the philosophy of Lao-Tsu, as anyone can see who reads A. C. Bouquet's *Sacred Books of the World* (Pelican, 1954), in the extracts from the Tao-te-King.

In the very beginning of the chaos produced from the 'big bang', all the elements which we can see as having emerged in evolution, and which are still emerging, were there. Anything that we recognise as existing now must have been there in the beginning, in however a tenuous form. Consciousness, thought, spontaneity, and of course the life-principle, were all there. 'In the world nothing could ever burst forth as final across the different thresholds successively traversed by evolution (however critical they be) which has not already existed in an obscure and primordial way.'[1]

The picture which emerges is an interesting one, because it gives an analogical description of the conflicting psychological forces within personality. The 'explosion' or rebellion is the force which encourages self-assertion, independence, separation. But there remains in the separated fragments the original tendency to coherence. Things and people tend to reunite in groups – from atoms to personalities: and this is the principle of Mind, which Empedocles and Anaxagoras, two and a half millennia ago, saw as the principle of order and creation. In more modern phraseology, in an expanding universe in which everything is rapidly becoming further and farther away from everything else there is the gravitational attraction which holds together the galaxies, the lesser systems within them, and the stars themselves.

This picture might indeed be a depressing one, if it were not that the principle of Mind, as it emerges, holds together this expanding universe in a single rational whole. The scope of mind is overtaking the expansion of matter (if one may still be allowed to use the word); and if Teilhard is right that we are on the brink of a break-through into something beyond the 'noosphere' – what he calls the *Hyperpersonal* – he would be justified in saying that as Mind has established a new coherence, so the new stage of the hyperpersonal will complete the 'collectivisation' of a scattered universe in a manner still incomprehensible to those who live on the plane of the noosphere.

[1] *Phenomenon*, p. 71.

It seems that in man alone Mind has become recognisable, because man alone can recognise it. But that does not mean that consciousness and self-consciousness are limited to man. It means that man is the point at which they have broken out from the 'within' and become unquestionable. Teilhard de Chardin points out that consciousness would be unique as a phenomenon, if it existed only at the point where it has been observed. It must have its extension in the cosmos. There must have been a primitive 'within' developing into a generalised consciousness and showing even in its early stages a certain limited spontaneity in its development. There must be a principle of uncertainty in a universe, which at best is only approximately predictable, and which grows less and less predictable the further evolution proceeds. No doubt Heisenberg's Principle of Indeterminacy is not something on which to base a philosophical theory, but at least the general abandonment of a mechanistic view of physics is more favourable to the kind of thinking encouraged by Teilhard when he examines the 'within'.

The examination of the 'within' will be much more troublesome than that of the 'without'; because in examining the 'without' we are observing three dimensions from the fourth; but the 'within' is that fourth dimension of thought and time in which we live. We ourselves are on the stage, and we can no longer even pretend to be objective.

The importance of Teilhard's concept of the 'within' is that it becomes something more than a mere concept. Rather in the same way as C. G. Jung begs his readers to believe that unconscious forces are as real as the things we touch and see, Teilhard insists again and again that the 'within' is none the less real for being not yet observable. It is indeed an emerging reality, best understood in terms of the two aspects of Time.

The 'without' of Time is successional, whether conceived as a straight line of things in a meaningless order (H. A. L. Fisher's view), or as a perpetual swing to and fro (Chinese philosophy, Hegel, Marx, Toynbee), or as a circular or spiral (Jains, Stoics, Spengler). The 'within' of Time is duration, which cannot be measured by any clock or calendar, because it depends on consciousness. Entry into the 'within' of Time is not reserved for mystics and Hindu holy men, because every human being is conscious of periods when 'Time goes slowly', and other periods when Time gallops.

'Time travels in divers paces with divers persons. I'll tell you who Time ambles withal, who Time trots withal, who Time gallops withal, and who he stands still withal.'[1]

There is more substance in Rosalind's remark than her conceits can justify. There is more variation in sleep, when the 'without' is in abeyance, and a long dream may in fact take a few seconds, whereas eight good hours sleep may feel like a moment of abstraction to a tired man.

The most recent observable product of the 'within', Teilhard insists, is the noosphere, which (with all that it implies) is distilled in the form of consciousness out of the process. The 'without' then becomes the whole length of past time – the part of the process which has become observable. The 'within' is the future, equally real but not yet observable, and always conditioned by the unpredictability which is itself part of the emerging reality.

This suggests something very significant about reality. In the noosphere reality is conditioned by Mind exercising free choice; so that reality looks like a landscape which is being traversed. What is ahead is fixed, but the course to be taken is free. Time then appears to be actual in the sense that no human being can stand on the emerging landscape: but in the noosphere Time is potential because it is the sphere of opportunity. The two senses of Time therefore seem to correspond with Teilhard's two energies. Radial energy causes the landscape of the future to unroll, and the individual may well roll along uneventfully over it for long periods; indeed, he must roll one way or another. Tangential energy is the individual's exploitation of opportunity. Radial energy is the eternal process with all its variety of possible choices: it is

[1] *As you like it:* Act III. Sc. 11.

4

energy on the level of quantity. Tangential energy is demonstrated in the series of choices made within the variety of possibles which build up a personality: it is energy on the level of quality. Radial energy is Hegel. Tangential energy is Kierkegaard.

Teilhard's most criticised weakness, on the levels of theology and philosophy, is a defect inherent in his most attractive quality, his optimism. Although his concept of tangential energy provides an opening for the forces of evil, he does not sufficiently emphasise evil itself. In a paper in this symposium Dr R. B. Smith shows convincingly that Teilhard does not leave out the problem of evil, but none the less most readers of *The Phenomenon* will feel that he nowhere really faces it. It is not enough to say that the element of unpredictability which issues eventually in human freewill solves the problem – that element which in the 'without' appears in the quantum and the principle of indeterminancy, and in the 'within' as tangential energy. The 'groping' in the stages of evolution which is an inevitable part of natural selection argues a kind of (metaphysical?) barrier set up. The enormous wastefulness of nature in the progress of life: the conflict and savagery of the law 'eat or be eaten': the destructiveness of natural cataclysms precipitated by nothing which can be even remotely associated with human error or wickedness: all these things corroborate the recurrent intuition of poets and prophets of almost every one of the known religions that the world is out of joint; and the complementary intuition of philosophers from Anaxagoras onwards that it is the duty of Mind (whether in gods or men) to set that disorder right.

In fact reason and religion have a duty to wage uncompromising and continual war with the spirit of misrule – whether capital or small S for spirit. But this spirit of misrule has a kind of order of its own: it has rules within its misrule. Clearly enough natural laws preserve a kind of approximate balance and achieve a sort of progress. But the course which these natural laws follow is one which reason cannot wholly approve, since it involves a ruthlessness opposite to an element which has come to the surface with the noosphere – the quality of mercy. But mercy itself can only successfully oppose the ruthlessness of natural law by developing another element – the quality of fortitude. This again can only successfully grow in the existential quality of trust; and since the natural order can provide nothing wholly trustworthy, reason has to look beyond it.

This reason can do, if it can find anything in the past which offers, not proof, but possible and reasonable ground for trust. Above all, if historical research can produce a personality or personalities, who have achieved freedom from the fears and resentments of life, then human reason can claim a ground for trust in a Something or Someone beyond or behind or beneath (spatial metaphors do not matter) the ruthless natural order.

But rebellion against the natural order, against ordinary society, with its perpetual plans to make itself fit the natural order, must inevitably produce a sense of guilt. This sense of guilt is something with which we have to come to terms. Kierkegaard noticed it but never came to terms with it: indeed he regarded the possibility of coming to terms with it as a temptation of the devil. Heidegger insisted that this very sense of guilt was a proper part of existential life. Man must face it, act in spite of it and endure conflict, which Heracleitus told men two and a half millennia ago was not only part of life but life itself.

Those who heard or read Sir Peter Medawar's Reith lectures (1959), 'The Future of Man', will not easily forget his uncompromising denial of genetic evolution, as shown in the world up to date, as an essentially good process. The fantastic errors of nature, as seen in Darwinian evolution, are things to be faced and acknowledged. The wasteful process of natural selection is not to be identified with the purpose of a divine designer. With the emergence of Mind through the development of brain a new type of evolution has come into action which, unlike the old, has a Lamarckian look.[1] The really dangerous thinkers are

'those who have attempted to graft a Darwinian or purely

[1] P. Medawar, *The Future of Man* (Methuen, 1960), p. 98.

elective interpretation upon the newer, non-genetical evolution of mankind'.[1]

Père Teilhard was not one of these, and Medawar – with all his scorn – prefers him to the neo-Darwinian. Teilhard does at least leave an opening for cosmic evil in the earliest stages of the process in his concept of the two energies: whether for good or evil, tangential energy must be a break-away from the regular order of nature. Yet I am sure that we are not to lay all the blame on tangential energy. In human beings, evil is not in free-will, but in freewill misused; nor can the whole of cosmic evil be blamed on his misuse of it. For while the Paradise Lost story was a great theological convenience to those who could in their day accept it, there are few who can sincerely use it as an escape route today. The usual mistake has, however, been made: in rejecting Paradise Lost as history, unthinking Christians reject it altogether. The early Church did not overpress the historicity of the story, though the Fathers probably believed it – there was no reason at the time why they should not have done. What they did press was its meaning. A glance through the passages quoted under Adam in the Patristic Greek Lexicon[2] shows clearly that Adam was defined as something very near to what was later called *Anima mundi*. They saw him as the ordered spirit of a totum: his name signified the world, its four elements and its four quarters, each letter standing for one of the four. In his misuse of freedom therefore the whole Totum fell into disorder. The fall of Adam is the cosmic Fall, in which Mind or Soul is fragmented: the Babel story gives a vivid picture of this in a second myth; and the whole history of the world is of its re-creation, so that the Spirit of Earth can regain order and unity.

This mythological picture is recognisably like the evolving world of Teilhard, but his failure to come to terms with the idea of the Fall leaves us with a Creator Spirit content to

[1] P. Medawar, *The Future of Man* (Methuen, 1960), p. 99.

[2] *The Patristic Greek Lexicon*, ed. G. W. H. Lampe (Oxford: Clarendon Press, 1961–68).

work in the ruthless and savage way of nature, without any suggestion to account for this apparently blind and clumsy method.

This is a weakness; but Teilhard was not setting out a complete system of theology. Yet we must notice what he loses by this weakness. If there is no Fall, there is no redemption directly connected with the cross of Christ: atonement simply becomes a gradual coordination of elements, and Christ almost becomes identified with the Holy Spirit, working from creation to point Omega. The cross is only the symbol of a groaning and suffering world: the concept of personal forgiveness is lost, or at least obscured. And if we have lost forgiveness we have lost Christ. It is not a matter of forgiveness only for ourselves as individuals, important though that may be. Forgiveness is cosmic: not only the cement of the Christian society, but the motive power of the whole process.

Evolution is creative, but it is also re-creative: creative first and foremost, because the work of re-creation goes beyond mere restoration: forgiveness produces in the creative process something better than could ever have been without it, because the process is irreversible. It is like a man weaving the pattern in a carpet and making several mistakes. He redeems the muddle not by undoing and starting afresh, but by quadrupling the size of the carpet and answering the mistakes with similar irregularities in the new quarters, until at last the carpet lies perfect and symmetrical. The Christian believes that God achieves perfection by addition and never by subtraction.

But no analogy may be pressed too far. The carpet parable breaks down if we let it suggest that there could be a static end to re-creative evolution. There is no 'final state', nor is there any scriptural promise to suggest one. The reward of faithful servants is to be set to new and exciting tasks, cities to be ruled over, tribes to be judged. If anyone supposes that to sit on thrones judging the tribes of Israel is a soft job, they should read the Old Testament. As T. W. Manson said, 'the reward of service will be more service'; and that service is to be the re-creative service of a forgiveness which continually redeems the past not by return and recollection, but by new adventures into the future – a future which continues the emergence of the 'within' (the potential) into actuality.

But what is actuality? It is primarily the plane of the observable, on which things are analysed and observed not subjectively (i.e. by the mind of the single person who conceives them), but objectively by the minds of a number of other people. Until they have been observed, analysed and valued, they can be said only to be ready to become actual: they could have been valued if there had been minds to assess them. Thus it is possible to see indefinite ages of the past being given value and definition by the minds of present-day men, not merely by the recognition of those ages as having been, nor in the mere accumulation of knowledge about them, but through the use of that knowledge for the direction of the future.

This is the function of the new dimension of Mind. The power which underlies the function is forgiveness, and the function itself is redemption. Forgiveness is the answer to regretted sin, and redemption is rescue from the situation into which sin has led. It is quite easy to see what we would call 'sin' active in evolution, with its cruelty and waste: but we see it because moral values have emerged with the emergence of Mind.

Before there were moral values it is difficult to see that cruelty and waste has real meaning. Until Mind sets up a pattern of what *ought* to be, cruelty and waste are simply parts of the way things are – neither good nor bad. It is Mind with its sense of ought-ness that calls nature's way evil because it does not conform to that ought-ness; and it finally decides that its own progress shall no longer be in nature's way, but according to certain moral laws. So Mind brings good out of an evil that was not of its own creating: it forgives the forces of evolution without condoning them. This agrees with the patristic view of Man in Christ as the cosmic redeemer: God in Christ redeems man, Man in Christ redeems nature. In this way the birth of the noosphere becomes not merely the culmination of the creative process up to date, but the potential deliverance of a world which has been travailing in pain until now, awaiting the redemption:[1] potential, because the deliverance waits upon man's own decision, which in its turn waits upon man's unanimity.

Such unanimity needs to be more than just horizontal. The web of the noosphere, covering the world, has to be more than just a web. Teilhard sees it as following the lines of spiritual longitude, to unite inevitably at the polar point Omega. But man's unanimity must without question extend into the history of his past and so integrate itself as well as into his purpose for the future.

This is the point at which Teilhard's emphasis is at its most valuable. Man's mind can only forgive and redeem the past by knowing it, by analysing it to see what were the seeds of progress. The point which a process has reached may be both interesting and relevant, but unless something is known of the direction along which it has travelled to reach that point, and the conditions precedent to its being-what-it-is, nothing of importance can be predicted. So Teilhard establishes the general direction of evolution by study of the past (the 'without') and predicts the probable future on the basis of that direction. He sees that direction as a process of unfolding, the value of which depends not on the process but on what comes out of it; and what is going to come out of it can be predicted to some extent by the study of the past and its implications.[2]

In study of the past man uses successional time as a yardstick: he estimates the age of his home, the planet Earth, in terms of years conveniently measured by its movement round the sun. But those years were never experienced as duration as far as the planet was concerned, because there was nobody to experience them. To think of them as duration is

[1] Romans 8:22 f.
[2] Cf. P. Medawar, *The Art of the Soluble* (Methuen, 1968), pp. 39–58. Teilhard here comes very near to Herbert Spencer's *Law of General Evolution*. Medawar does not recognise such a law, or even a General Evolution, though he is much kinder to Spencer than to Père Teilhard.

therefore false in any sense except one. To man now they can be *imagined* as duration by the device of exporting his own time-sense into a period in which there was no time-sense.

This is not simply Berkeleian philosophy without God. Berkeley without God would be a disaster, and I have deliberately taken an anthropocentric position which neither pre-supposes nor denies the Christian God. But even without God we need not deny reality to phenomena because there is no contemporary mind to appreciate them. Yet we are bound to say that duration time is an aspect of reality which only exists provided that there is a mind to evaluate it. In fact, duration time is only a phenomenon when there is a someone to whom it is shown. The 'things' themselves have a limited reality which is confirmed by the discovery of their traces. Their duration has a limited reality when assessed by the minds of men reaching back into a past which can be measured on the yardstick of successional time. This sets them in a certain evolutionary order useful for comparison but utterly unreal in terms of experience. This order and development can be imagined, and its probability corroborated by evidence; but when we speak of it as a 'long' period, we do not mean that any finite mind knew it as long: merely that by comparison with our own period measured in successional time it would have seemed long if we had been there.

Since any picture of past or future involves a degree of identification with that picture, the picture will necessarily be false. The picture of the past is built on a foundation of induction from existing phenomena; therefore it is a picture with an observer who has imported into it a time-sense and a set of values alien to the picture-in-itself.

By his insistence on a primitive 'within', however, even in the earliest stages, Teilhard gives a certain reality to the values imported from the present into a still mindless past. The 'within', containing the seeds of mind, justifies our use of moral terms such as good, evil, right, wrong, cruel, disastrous, into our vocabulary in describing the early stages of the biosphere and even into the ages of pre-life.

This is what justifies his use of the term orthogenesis as a proper description of a line of progress along which granulation, life, consciousness, reflection, religion and morals gradually emerge. The very incompleteness of the process invalidates condemnation of the method employed by nature – as a Christian will say – by God: *The Phenomenon* is not a theodicy. But it can properly be maintained that Teilhard's confidence (which Medawar calls euphoria) in the future has reasonable grounds. There will be a final unfolding and a final unanimity: to return to Anaxagoras, Mind having penetrated chaos will produce cosmos, in which everything will find its own place, not in any static sense, but in a final harmonious activity.

It remains to sum up Teilhard's profit and loss account, as I see it.

(*a*) His greatest virtue is his emphasis on quality as against quantity. The size and age of the universe are irrelevant for assessment of real value. Point Omega is all quality, not quantity; and point Omega is (for Christians) Christ. This resolves at once the more thick-headed objections to the idea of incarnation. Jesus Christ displayed God in terms of quality. One has heard learned (but not very profound) pleasantries on B.B.C. panels, suggesting a curiously blind spot in the minds of otherwise intelligent theologians who can believe that God was in Christ. But the blind spot is in those who fail to see the irrelevance of quantity as anything but a means. Teilhard manages to make this point without falling into the error of the Hermetists and later Neoplatonists, whose systems were all to some extent dualist. Teilhard is uncompromisingly monist; and if in one or two places he suggests that what is superfluous can be thrown away, one feels that this is not what he really means. His thesis must be that nothing real is lost, and that the whole evolutionary process belongs to reality. Earlier I have said that what matters is what comes out of the process, and the rest can go on the compost heap; and by this I tried to recognise that what is left behind in the process is not rubbish to be burned. A compost heap makes useful material out of refuse: it remains dynamic. Point Omega – the Christ quality – binds the whole together, and enables the redeemed universe to become fully dynamic in the sphere of perfection.

(b) Teilhard is always affirmative. Nothing is to him 'just' what it seems. The temptation of the specialist is to speak in those terms. Even Medawar, whose scope is very wide indeed, suggests that dreams may be 'just' noise. Teilhard never limits the function of anything to what he understands of it.

(c) He has robbed us of the right to pass particular moral judgments on the course of evolution.

(d) He has re-introduced us to the Bergsonian distinction between Time as succession, and Time as duration.

(e) His picture of the spread of the noosphere has a curiously sacramental look. Technology serves as its outward and visible sign. Contacts through war, even, can be hopeful symptoms of final unity on the way.

(f) While Teilhard is definitely monist, he recognises a duality in things-as-they-are. The motive power of the process is split: the release of free energy within the pattern of ordered energy has somehow got out of step. (I have written of this in a shorter essay, in which I have tried to show that the reconciliation of these is the key to final unity.)

On the other side, one must acknowledge gaps in Teilhard's account of evolution. I cannot presume, as a casual reader of scientific books within my scope, to make scientific criticisms; but there are philosophic awkwardnesses.

(a) In one way, Teilhard has started us off in the air. We are like Socrates in his basket, μετέωρος as the Greeks have it. While giving us a fully cosmic Christ in a teleological sense (point Omega) he has left us to pre-suppose something pre-cosmic to account for an apparently mindless and a-moral universe, in which the redeeming factor has been so thoroughly dissipated that it can only emerge with fantastic difficulty and through aeons of successional time. What was it made the original mess?

(b) While showing that the motive power, which forms the energies which make progress towards unity, is Christian *agape* with its reconciling quality of forgiveness, Teilhard still

leaves us wondering whether it will be produced by compulsory conglomeration. He leaves one reader at least with
the feeling that he had made too little of the emergency, in
spite of references to our responsibility.

(c) This is perhaps because he makes too little of the
increasing speed of development in science and technology
– or, we might say, the increasing speed of duration time –
and the consequent imbalance between the 'without' and the
'within'.

(d) His answer to the problem of increasing leisure does
not satisfy, in spite of a notable remark about boredom as the
chief danger to society. Surely no one but a man who had
lived most of his life among highly intelligent minds could
suppose that most men and women were capable of employ-
ing their new leisure on research.

But, having made these criticisms, let it be said that
Teilhard asked for criticism and welcomed it. Nor is it true
to say, as Sir Peter Medawar has said, that 'this reconciliation' (between the supernatural and the natural) 'is just what
Teilhard's book is *about!*'[1] (his italics and exclamation mark)
That was part of it, but not even the most of it. It was far
more importantly to cure this melancholic age of its death-
wish: euphoria perhaps, but why not? 'All shall be well, and
all shall be well, and all manner of things shall be well.' He
has given a reasonable hope to numbers of people who were
in danger of losing hope. He presents an intelligible picture
of the past; and he insists rightly that whether we prefer to
call the process Chance or Design (the label on the bottle is
not the thing that matters most) there has been a meaningful
direction in evolution. This process has turned a number of
uncomfortable corners against all probability in the past, and
will do so again through the exercise of the new power of
Mind, with its accompanying qualities of courage, com-
passion and insight.

He makes no secret of what it is that chiefly gives him
ground for this hope (a good sturdy Christian hope, this – no
pale spectre of the betting-shop). It is that whereas evolution

[1] P. Medawar, *The Art of the Soluble*, p. 81.

has so far been carried along by *vis a tergo*, it is now being drawn forward by a vision which, in spite of its different look to different people, is really One, personal and dynamic: and this is a Christ whose concern goes beyond my salvation or man's salvation, for he is the cosmic Christ.

SIX

Incarnation: The Reconciliation of the Energies

H. A. BLAIR

It could be said that whereas orthodox Christianity hangs on three main points, creation, restoration and a final climax, Père Teilhard's general concept hangs on two only: it stretches from creation directly to the final climax. It is not that he ignores the gospel story or discounts the work and sacrifice of Christ, but rather that he takes them in as part of the creative process leading to that final climax. His gaze is fixed so firmly on Christ as the end (point Omega) that he has no time for Christology or Chalcedonian formulae.

In a sense this is because he was so convinced of the part played by Christ from beginning to end. He saw him as the Word, the Wisdom and the Life: the cosmic Christ is the dynamic of existence. In making this emphasis he inevitably under-emphasised the need for reconciliation of conflicting forces in the process, of which Christ was the dynamic: at least, in as far as he recognised the need of reconciliation he seems to have seen it as part of the continuing process of creation.

Theology at all stages and in all properly Christian schools of thought has recognised the incarnation as the perfect example of freedom. Whether we regard the 'new theologians' of the 1960s as *avant garde*, or as deserters, at least they cannot be accused of not recognising this. Jesus was the man psychologically free, unbound by environment because dependent on God; but at the same time he was conscious of being involved in, and to that extent bound by, the society of his day. His freedom was limited by his human condition. What then is freedom?

Dr Leonard Hodgson in his Gifford lectures describes two freedoms, which he calls freedom (a) and freedom (b). Freedom (a) is the unrestricted freedom of the will:

> 'Certain organisms, when they have arrived at a certain kind of complexity of constitution, find themselves conscious not only of being the subjects of the experiences that come to them through their bodies, but also able to choose between different courses of action in a world of causation, contingency and purpose.'[1]

But contingency is an irrationality, and therefore intolerable in a world governed by causation; freedom to alter direction must therefore cause havoc. On the other hand, freedom (a) does not in fact exist in the world as we know it. All freedom of choice is modified and redirected and sometimes completely blocked by environment, as well as by inherent limitations in the character which makes the choice.

The only serviceable freedom therefore in the world as we know it is freedom (b), which is the kind of freedom limited by the physical weaknesses of the subject, and by the awkwardnesses of the environment. This we could describe as freedom incarnate, which Christians believe they see exemplified perfectly in the figure of Jesus between birth and death. This freedom is conceivable and reconcilable with reason, while freedom (a) is inconceivable, and its existence is bound to be a matter of faith. But freedom (b) depends on the existence of freedom (a), its presupposition. A thing cannot be modified and limited unless it exists.

This was the difficulty of the existentialists, led by Kierkegaard, who fought to the death (quite literally) the Hegelian attempt to rationalise the transcendental, and the Church's betrayal of her trust (as he saw it) in becoming a party to this theology of synthesis:

[1] Leonard Hodgson, *For Faith and Freedom* (S.C.M., 1968), p. 173.

'The majority of men. . . live and die under the impression that life is simply a matter of understanding more and more, and that if it were granted to them to live longer, life would continue to be one long continuous growth in understanding. How many of them ever experience the maturity of discovering that there comes a critical moment where everything is reversed, after which the point becomes to understand more and more that there is something which cannot be understood?

That is Socratic ignorance, and that is what the philosophy of our times requires as a corrective.'[1]

Teilhard did not try to rationalise in the sense of explaining the inconceivable: but he was concerned to open a door between those who disowned anything beyond the empirical, and those who dismissed the empirical as valueless for conveying a valid picture of reality. The key to this door, for him, was a picture of evolution as the emergence of mind, bringing with it freedom of choice and hope for the future.

Freedom limited by flesh produces tension: tension, or strife as Heracleitus called it, produces life.[2] A more cumbersome modern term is the principle of complementarity. As applied to the logical processes it leads to reflection which follows the birth of the Noosphere. Sir Peter Medawar (who has no love for Père Teilhard) has called this the transition from selective development to instructive development.[3] It is not the dawn of freedom, because there is some freedom evident in the creature's ability to select from alternatives: but it is the birth of a new freedom, by which the creatures are no longer limited to a few alternatives, but can give instructions which alter their environment to suit themselves.

These instructions are the result of reflection which is the result of tension. There are certain instructions which the

[1] *The Journals of Kierkegaard*. Transl. Alexander Dru (Fontana, 1958), p. 172.

[2] *Heracleitus, fragment* 80. Translated in F. M. Cornford, *Greek Religious Thought* (Dent, 1923), p. 84.

[3] P. Medawar, *The Future of Man* (Methuen, 1960), Ch. 6 *passim*.

new creature, equipped with reflection, cannot give, because through reflection he recognises the limits of his new freedom and accepts them. But when his reflection gives him no certainty of what those limits are, he does not sink into a sort of vegetable apathy but makes experiment. The resulting tension produces further reflection and ultimately decision.

Freedom has therefore gone hand in hand with limitation and has advanced one step nearer to truth, which it could not have done without that limitation. Scientific progress is therefore bound up with freedom incarnate.

But intuitional truth does not seem to be bound up with limitation in the same way: in fact physical limitation often causes distortion, and the reflecting subject has resort again to experiment if the proposition is of a kind which can be verified.

Verification can be empirical or evidential. The verification which establishes something as a working hypothesis for the scientist will be of the laboratory or observatory type, and will provide a platform for further research. Evidential verification will be of the law-court type, the testimony of witnesses. The first kind of verification is concerned with the nature of things, the second with principles for living. The first deals with statements, the second gives directions with a moral tone.

It seems therefore that the process arising from freedom and its limitation (and consequent tension) is useful: (*a*) for keeping open the way towards the understanding of a universe which demands to be understood, but of which no final understanding is ever possible because of its continual change; (*b*) for establishing principles of living within that universe on the evidence of those who have had experiences of it not limited to those capable of verification. For there are propositions which, as Wittgenstein has pointed out, belong to unverifiable categories. There are also propositions which could only prove false, because they are by definition unverifiable and unique. To 'prove' them would be to prove them not to be what we had supposed they were.

This might suggest at first glance that the dogma of the

scientist was good and useful as providing a firm platform for the next jump forward, but that religious or ethical dogma was not. In fact that is not quite true: the scientist should be dogmatic within his always conscientious limits, because his indicative statements are more than just jumping-off places for further exploration: they are also implied pieces of advice and warnings to society. Yet society is too often left in ignorance not only of what his statements imply but of the content of the statements themselves. It is therefore the duty of the religious or ethical teacher to know something of what the scientist is saying, and to relate those statements to the sphere of conduct and worship. Here at once is produced tension between the freedom of the spirit and the limitation of the flesh: but I am proposing that the only true freedom is freedom with tension, because freedom comes of truth, which is itself the child of that same tension.

The fact, therefore, that the religious or ethical teacher cannot prove his statements by experiment, but only show them reasonable and then call his witnesses, does not absolve him from using the imperative. His kind of evidence does not even entitle him to say, 'This turned out badly last time, therefore I must not advise it again'; because he is forbidden to judge by visible short term results. G. E. Moore has shown all too clearly the danger of trying to base ethical principles on pragmatic ground. At what point are you going to stop reckoning the chain of cause and effect? You have pulled the emergency cord and stopped the train because the mother of the child in your carriage who had stepped out to buy a paper had been too long, the train had started without her and the small child panicked and became hysterical. By so doing you made five business men late for their appointments, and one surgeon consultant arrived too late for an emergency appendicitis – which punctured and the patient died. Yet who can say categorically that you made the wrong decision? How far are your critics to follow results before they condemn you? Were the business appointments for the good of society or for the profit of the few? Was death perhaps the best result for that patient? Would the three-year-old's panic, if prolonged, have caused a permanent trauma, affecting the rest of her life – and through her, those of her family? Yet none of those unanswered questions affect the right of the naval officer in the same compartment to be dogmatic when the guard arrives and say that you did the proper thing because *quick action in emergency is vital*. The guard (who says that you were wrong) is full of righteousness and radial energy. His ethics are wrapped up in regularity and rules. You however made your tangential decision, and felt very indignant when it cost you 25 pounds. The naval officer in effect reconciled what are the two energies of Père Teilhard, the radial and the tangential, by insisting that you had acted on a principle compatible with both. Your decision had turned a corner and presented a new landscape, in a way which your previous actions that day had not done. Your morning bath, your breakfast, your taxi to the station and your choice of a compartment had not been real decisions and were almost automatic. But when the moment of decision did arrive, you made it.

One remembers T. S. Eliot's 'The Family Reunion', and Agatha's remark:

'At this moment there is no decision to be made;
The decision will be made by powers beyond us
Which now and then emerge.'[1]

If you like to say it in Greek you will mention 'Chronos' and 'Kairos'. There are in fact two orders of time, one driven by radial, and one by tangential energy: the former is succession time, marked by clocks and calendars; the latter is duration time and is marked by decisions, whether of God or man.

This is as much as to say that a right decision at anything but the right time is no decision, or at least not a right one (so importing the moral tone). But can we see anything of this emphasis in Père Teilhard? Are there patterns in his

[1] T. S. Eliot, *The Family Reunion*. Part I, Scene 2, p. 50. (Faber, 7th impression, 1952).

thinking which suggest that significant decisions in the process (which he makes a parable of life) come spasmodically?

In *The Phenomenon* we find him repeatedly making the point that in spite of the 'automatic suppression of the peduncles' (our inability to see new beginnings at their beginnings) we everywhere get the impression that each new beginning has its moment, and that no other moment will do. There is always a moment when light breaks, the kettle boils, the cells form; and various reasons combine to suggest that the coming of life was a 'once-for-all', and is not a rhythmic pulsation repeated at intervals. But he also comments on the late arrival of life in succession time; yet succession time is what we associate with radial energy, of which the speed does not vary. He also comments on the immense length of the early periods, and the quickening tempo as evolution proceeds: and as the indeterminate principle becomes more and more noticeable, and 'corners' which the process seems to turn come more often. These 'corners' are the tangential moments which break away from regularity, continuity and the kind of orderliness beloved of head clerks. This general concept of the two processes breaking in on each other has found a place in many of the ancient religions, but without (so far as I know) the suggestion that the tempo of irregularity is increasing.

It was not, I think, to account for the ruthlessness of nature that Père Teilhard introduced the concept of two energies, radial and tangential: and it would be a meaningless question to ask which of them is the good, and which the bad form of energy, since both are quite necessary. Yet some readers of his work have done just that: they have assumed that radial energy is the 'love that makes the world go round', which is interrupted and thrown out of gear by the vagaries of tangential energy. On the other hand Heidegger seems to suggest that existential being is only established by the repeated break away from the regularity of life, and the endurance (bravely) of the inevitable sense of guilt. Meanwhile some of Teilhard's champions have answered the challenge of Christian critics that there is no 'Fall' doctrine in his system by pointing at tangential energy as itself a kind of Fall.

In fact, both energies are good: their oppositions are good, because without them nothing would be created: with only one of them the universe would be either anarchy or the world of Ecclesiastes – a world of pure survivalism.

But there is a right question to ask: why do not the two energies keep step? There are other questions. Why do the 'moments' (or 'corners') sometimes sccm to have been explosive? Why was it necessary for one kind of life – that of a star – to peter out before a new kind of life could break through? Would it not have been better arranged if the two forms of energy had kept running shoulder to shoulder, instead of the one form getting a long lead of several laps and then being overhauled by the other form (tangential) lap after lap at increasing speed? If there is a finish, will they finish together? and what if they do? Is this point Omega? I would suggest that this is the reconciliation, in which all mistaken decisions find forgiveness. When they find their right places in Time they find their proper order.

This is no original idea, since it was present in the thought of many eastern Fathers. We remember Papias, quoted by Andreas of Caesarea:

'To some of them (clearly the angels which at first were holy) he gave dominion also over the arrangement of the universe, and he commissioned them to exercise their dominion well. (And he says next:) But it so befell that their array came to nought; for the great dragon . . . was cast down to earth, he and his angels.'[1]

Tatian also speaks of fallen spirits, which like letters in a manuscript have lost all meaning through disorder.[2] We might go further than Tatian, and see disorder not as something meaningless, but like a gigantic anagram – a rearrangement of the letters conveying a false meaning.

[1] J. B. Lightfoot, *The Apostolic Fathers;* one vol. edn. (Macmillan, 1893), pp. 521, 532.
[2] Tatian, *adv. Graecos*, 17.

The same thought appears in early Greek philosophy:
'Mind set in order all things as they were to be, and as they
were (before) but now have ceased to be, and as they
are. . . .'[1]

In this thought of Anaxagoras, the superiority of Mind
depends on its complete unmixedness with the things which
it arranges. Because of its independence, its decisions are
objective and unaffected by environment. Its freedom is (as
Dr Hodgson has put it) freedom (a): it is an absolute freedom
of absolute Mind, not (like that of Virgil's Aeneas) a divided
one. Freedom (b) is a divided freedom, because every
decision depends upon the situation in which it is made.

So in the Hindu philosophy of the Vedanta, with its
monism, we find the principle of the Advaita: that the One
is right and true (and the Many are reconcilable in the One)
but the Two are always wrong. Here, and in all forms of
Eastern religion which witness to man's intuition of truth as
Unity and not Duality, we have the same demand for
reconciliation in the One. The Many cannot find unity until
'the two are one'.

Which two? Here the religions speak with many voices,
in terms of light and darkness, life and death, faith and
knowledge, time and eternity, freedom and destiny. No truth
is to be found in the rejection of one and acceptance of
another: it is in the reconciliation of the two that the true
unity is to be found, after which the disordered 'many' will
slip into place.

I need hardly point out how closely this corresponds to the
picture of Jesus Christ in the gospels. St Paul continually
hammers at the idea of Jesus as the man 'who is our peace,
who has made us both one and has broken down the dividing
wall of hostility',[2] in whom 'all things hold together.'[3]
For Paul, as for Père Teilhard, the ultimate division is
between man and God, and this has caused the separations

[1] F. M. Cornford, op. cit., *Anaxagoras, fragment* 12, pp. 124 f.
[2] Ep. to the Ephesians, 2:14.
[3] Ep. to the Colossians, 1:17.

which appear so clearly in the world. So Jew and Gentile, both searching for God, are only reconciled in Christ: Law and Freedom, both directing towards the human 'good life', are reconciled in Love.

The hates, the enmities, the fears and suspicions are merely symptoms of conflicting energies, designed as opposites but not antagonists; complementary and not incompatible.

It is time itself that is out of joint, though the over-quotation of Hamlet's words has robbed them of much of their impact. Greek tragedy illustrated the theme, in which two forces meet, neither wholly bad and both with elements of greatness. The tension between them brings one wrong decision as a result of which none of the following decisions can possibly be right: one disastrous decision after another brings the moment when the tension is finally resolved at tremendous cost. We end with a stage littered with corpses and a curious sense that evil has been purged.

In the figure of Jesus, however, we have not the tragic solution. As he fits the two energies and the two time-series together, we see a man most particular to keep to the regularities of succession time and radial energy, until the right moment appears. This is clearest in the fourth gospel, but it is there in all the gospels. He will keep the Law until the emergency demands its extension or revision. He will save the situation at the wedding feast, but not at a moment chosen by anyone else – even his mother. He will go up to Jerusalem, but not at his brothers' dictation: he will await the 'kairos'.

Without then making any attempt to explain the disjointedness of the two energies, Teilhard sees them as not yet in harmony. This is surely the point at which he would have placed the Fall, if he had written on it; not in tangential energy, nor in radial energy, but in the rift between them. The turning in of Time on itself at the Omega point is nothing less than the harmonising and reconciling of a dynamic which has gone berserk because it has split, and which can only find its harmony in Christ (speaking in personal terms), in Love (speaking in moral values), in harmony and order (speaking, like Pythagoras, in terms of music and mathematics). At this point the freedom of the Spirit becomes incarnate in ordered and disciplined flesh: in fact God becomes Man in Christ.

SEVEN

Teilhard de Chardin and Modern Protestant Theology

W. J. P. BOYD

To some it appears that Teilhard was so seriously isolated by the prohibitions laid upon him by the Holy Office, that he was 'forced to thrash around in the circle of his own ideas, without the benefit of serious criticism, and hence without making real contact with either the science or the theology he cared about so deeply'.[1] There is truth in this judgment which provokes speculation about the difference it might have made not only to Teilhard, but also to his era of theology, if from the first there had been the freest interchange and expression of ideas. It might seem, therefore, that it would be more appropriate to compare his theology with that of orthodox Roman Catholic theology. In fact, we have such comparisons from Roman Catholic scholars, both appreciative and critical. Friends and members of his own society have contributed valiant defences of his theological orthodoxy; their works are valuable and illuminating.[2] The only query which these sympathetic treatments raise is the wonderment why there ever was a ban on his religious and

[1] J. Habgood, in a review in *Theology*, lxx, 563, p. 231 f.
[2] To mention some of the more outstanding available in English: Henri de Lubac, *The Religion of Teilhard de Chardin* (Collins, 1967); Émile Rideau, *Teilhard de Chardin: A guide to his thought* (Collins, 1967); C. F. Mooney, *Teilhard de Chardin and the mystery of Christ* (Collins, 1966); N. M. Wildiers, *An introduction to Teilhard de Chardin* (Fontana, 1968). For a critical assessment of Teilhard, see Olivier Rabut, *Dialogue with Teilhard de Chardin* (Sheed and Ward, 1961).

theological writing, if it is so basically sound. The value, then, of looking at Teilhard's work through Protestant theological spectacles is that it readjusts the perspective and enables us to see that despite his isolation, he is none the less sensitive to the currents of thought and theological needs of his time, and is already asking the same questions as Protestant theologians and tackling similar problems. He himself was not all that conscious of his own isolation, as the following passage reminds us:

'Because I am conscious of having a very intense awareness of the aspirations deep at the heart of my age (as others have of the miseries), I feel it my duty to bear this testimony before my brothers in the apostolate. . . .'[1] In his essay, 'Mon Univers', dated 1924, written in Tientsin,[2] Teilhard feels his identity with the intellectual life of his times sufficiently to be able to describe himself as 'an ordinary man of the twentieth century', who was able to share 'as anyone else would in the ideas and cares of his own time. . . .' Such passages may lead us to ask whether Teilhard's theological development was a unique, spiritual pilgrimage, or whether in the development of his ideas we find close affinities with modern theological thought, produced by a common reaction to the new scientific knowledge, and the pressures and needs of the modern world. In a sense both alternatives are true of him. There was real isolation, movingly expressed in an essay, 'Le Christique', written in 1955 shortly before his death:[3] 'How does it happen that, still intoxicated by my vision, I look all around me and find myself practically alone? How is it that I alone should have seen? How is it that I am incapable if someone asks me, of citing a single author, a single work, where there is to be found clearly expressed that marvellous "diaphany" which in my eyes has transfigured everything? . . . May I not after all be simply the victim of some mental delusion? That is what I ask

[1] This letter is cited by C. F. Mooney, op. cit., p. 192.
[2] This essay is published in *Science and Christ* (Collins, 1968), p. 37.
[3] *Le Christique* is not yet published, but this extract is cited by C. F. Mooney, pp. 196 f.

myself.' And yet, as we read his works, we find him sensitive to modern problems and clearly enunciating themes which characterise modern theology.

I

Whilst the main concern of this essay is to compare Teilhard's christology with that of Dietrich Bonhoeffer and Paul Tillich, a brief comment may be allowed about the modern cast of his theology generally. Bishop John Robinson's *Honest to God* brought home to millions of readers that in modern theology the emphasis upon immanence as the way in which we ought to think about God was so serious that there was the greatest difficulty in attaching any intelligible meaning to the concept of transcendence.[1] In Teilhard's christology we find a tremendous emphasis upon immanence. True enough, he does not abandon transcendence, but the heavy emphasis is upon immanence. We see that in his strong protest against a 'juridical' christology. By this I mean that Teilhard was repelled by the idea that Jesus Christ has the right to be called Lord and Son of God simply because God has declared him to be such. If his legal title to reign is attributable simply to God's fiat, then the lordship of Christ is compatible with any sort of world at all. Teilhard clearly feels that such an idea makes incarnation incredible. However, if incarnation has any serious meaning then it must be understood as physically and organically related to the deepest realities of life and the whole of matter.[2] Modern theology is also characterised by its affirmation of the world. Traditionally there has always been a world-denying element in Christianity: 'Do not love the world, neither the things that are in the world. If anyone loves the world, love for the Father

[1] Teilhard sounded the warning about the disappearance of transcendence in an important essay, 'Catholicism and Christ' written in Paris in 1946: 'With the universe rescued from immobility, a kind of divinity, completely immanent in the world, was progressively tending to take the place in man's consciousness of the transcendent Christian God,' *Science and Christ*, p. 188.

[2] Cf. the very able discussion of this aspect of Teilhard's thought by C. F. Mooney, pp. 78–87.

is not in him' (1 John 2:15). This theme has been powerfully reinforced in Christianity through the whole tradition of asceticism. Withdrawal from the world has been one of the chief targets of criticism in the work of such radical theologians as William Hamilton and T. J. J. Altizer in America. Hamilton re-defines twentieth century protestantism as the movement from cloister to world . . . '(which) means from church, from place of protection and security, of order and beauty, to the bustling middle-class world of the new university, of politics, princes and peasants'.[1] Whilst Teilhard was too mature to have a blind-spot to the deep, religious values of catholic asceticism, in which he had been nurtured, none the less he was not blind to its limitations, and in his writings he tackles the problem of how love for God can be reconciled with love for the world. This theme is to the fore-front of *Writings in Time of War*. In an essay, 'Mastery of the World and the kingdom of God' he endorses but qualifies 'the gospel precept that we must *contemn and hate the world*', agreeing that we should renounce the self-centred world, 'the world of pleasure, the damned portion of the world that falls back and worships itself';[2] yet if the Church is to make its true impact upon the world of our day, it will be so, as she is able to point out to life, 'her finest children busy in forwarding, side by side, mastery of the world and the kingdom of God'.[3] In his essay, 'The Heart of the Problem', Teilhard argues for the necessity and possibility of reconciling Marxist faith in the world and its future possibilities with Christian faith in a transcendent God: 'But let there be revealed to us the possibility of believing at the same time and wholly in God and the World, *the one through the other*.'[4] Although Teilhard's solution at this point differs from Altizer's solution, yet both men share the same concern to

---

[1] Cf. his essay, 'The death of God theologies today', published in *Radical Theology and the Death of God*, by T. J. J. Altizer and William Hamilton (Penguin, 1968), p. 48.

[2] *Writings in Time of War* (Collins, 1968), p. 90.

[3] *Ibid.*, p. 91.

[4] *The Future of Man* (Collins, 1964), pp. 268 f; the italics are mine.

discover God through the world.[1] There are many statements in Altizer's presentation with which Teilhard would
have been deeply sympathetic: Altizer pleads for a truly
human faith;[2] Teilhard pronounces the authority of the
Church as incomplete and ineffectual, 'to the extent that it
fails to embrace as it should *everything that is human on earth*'.[3]
Altizer concludes his book by telling us that 'the radical
Christian calls us into the centre of the world, into the heart
of the profane, with the announcement that Christ is present
here and he is present nowhere else. Once we confess that
Christ is fully present in the moment before us, then we can
truly love the world, and can embrace even its pain and
darkness as an epiphany of the body of Christ'.[4] Teilhard
declares his love for the world in no less emphatic terms but
also provides a solution to Altizer's problem. Altizer felt that
to believe in Christ's resurrection and ascension was to deny
his total commitment to incarnation. It was to reverse the
forward, constructive and redeeming movement of Christ
into the world. The death of God for Altizer means the total

---

[1] T. J. J. Altizer, *The Gospel of Christian Atheism* (Westminster Press,
Philadelphia, 1966), p. 10: 'Theology must seek the presence of Christ
in the world.'

[2] *Ibid.*, p. 19: 'In the past, theologians have dared to claim that nothing
which is human is foreign to faith. Can we make that claim? Can we go
beyond it and assert as a matter of principle that the most authentically
human is a manifestation of faith?' Compare Teilhard's statement in
The Making of a Mind (Collins, 1965), p. 186: 'May God give us, and
multiply their numbers, Christians who *in virtue of their religion*, will bear,
more than any other human creature, the burden of their own time's
aspirations and toil. Ah, if only we were able to instil into our charity
an egalitarian passion for the people. . . . More than anyone, our Lord
lived the life of men. . . .' 23 Feb. 1917.

[3] Cf. *The Future of Man*, p. 265. Teilhard diagnoses the malaise of
modern Christianity as due to its fundamental lack of 'the sensitising
ingredient of *human* faith and hope without which, in reason and in
fact, no religion can henceforth appear to Man other than colourless,
cold and inassimilable' (pp. 265 f.). Again he writes, '. . . but above
all we must, with all that is human within us, rethink our religion' –
Science and Christ, p. 126.

The Gospel of Christian Atheism, p. 156.

change in the life of God from being a remote, transcendent, wholly other-worldly Deity, to an incarnate, immanent being, at first concentrated in the life of Jesus of Nazareth, and then, released by the crucifixion, into the whole life of mankind. For such a view, clearly, resurrection and ascension can only be retrograde; and Altizer saw these latter concepts as a denial of the love of God for his world. Teilhard fully meets Altizer's contention that God must be thought of as loving the world and being totally committed to the world in a quite incontrovertible manner, by his own doctrine of irreversibility. He expounds this concept in such a way that he shows how it is possible to understand anew the concepts of transcendence and eternity without falling into the error and snare of oriental total world-renunciation. Only the concept of Omega can guarantee the sort of irreversibility for which Altizer pleads. Teilhard's doctrine of irreversibility has the merit of confirming what is true and valuable in Altizer's work, which has suffered from blanket condemnation by outraged orthodox theological opinion, and at the same time exposing its weakness of one-sided over-emphasis, by providing a more intellectually satisfying solution at this point.[1] The doctrine of irreversibility alone will enable a man to 'pledge himself in the service of the earth';[2] but such irreversibility in no sense requires a denial of resurrection and ascension, or of eternity and transcendence, rather, irreversibility demands them.

Another characteristic of modern theology is its emphasis upon the importance of personal relationships for the understanding of spiritual reality. Two very different books have this concern in common: *Honest to God* popularised the view of Jesus as 'the man for others': 'to say that "God is personal" is to say that . . . personality is of *ultimate* significance in the constitution of the universe, that in personal relationships

---

[1] Cf. the discussion of the doctrine of irreversibility in de Lubac, p. 181; *The Future of Man*, pp. 180 f, 206 f.

[2] Cf. *Writings in Time of War*, p. 79; and Isaiah 41:4, where 'with the last' implies that what God has created will endure; the Creator will not abolish his creation.

we touch the final meaning of existence as nowhere else'.[1] Similarly the remarkable Bampton lectures of David Jenkins[2] revolve around 'Concern for Persons' as the key concept for a proper understanding of christology, God and the world. Teilhard shares the same concern. He forthrightly denounces the Marxist view that the justification and true motivation of human effort is the legacy of achievement which the individual may bequeath to society, on the grounds of its utter inadequacy: 'in these contributions to the collectivity, far from transmitting the most precious, we are bequeathing, at the utmost, only the shadow of ourselves. Our works? But even in the interest of life in general, what is the effect of human works if not to establish, in and by means of each one of us, an absolutely original centre in which the universe reflects itself in a unique and inimitable way?'[3]

The logic of the argument demands that hope for the future must include a view of death, not as the destroyer of persons, but as the means whereby each personal centre is brought into true relationship with Omega, the centre of centres. Teilhard does not see the value of persons in purely an individualistic kind of way. For him, love means that persons are drawn together in the deepest way – that is, 'centre to centre'. He expounds: 'In our lives this centric condition is seldom achieved . . . it may be that in our human inter-relationships we come into contact with our fellows only "tangentially", through our interests, through our functions, or for our business dealings . . . without loving – without even suspecting that it is possible for us to love – the thing or person with which we are concerned. Thus our interior life remains fragmented and pluralised.'[4] Equally, Bishop Robinson writes: 'Life in Christ Jesus . . . means

[1] J. A. T. Robinson, *Honest to God* (S.C.M. paperback, 1963), pp. 48 f.

[2] David Jenkins, *The Glory of Man*, Bampton Lectures for 1966 (S.C.M., 1967).

[3] *The Phenomenon of Man* (Collins, 1959), p. 261.

[4] 'Super Humanity, Super-Christ, Super Charity', in *Science and Christ*, pp. 169 f.

having no absolutes but his love, being totally uncommitted in every other respect but totally committed in this. And this utter openness in love to the "other", for his own sake, is equally the only absolute for the non-Christian, as the Parable of the Sheep and Goats shows. He may not recognise Christ in the "other" but in so far as he has responded to the claim of the unconditional in love he has responded to him – for he is the "depth" of love.'[1]

Sufficient has been said to justify a comparison of Teilhard's thought with that of modern protestant theologians. We began, however, with a quotation which cast doubt on his competence in theology no less than in science. We must ask, then, two preliminary questions: 'Was Teilhard a theologian?' and secondly, 'If so, how should we classify his theology?' A fellow-Jesuit, the renowned Karl Rahner rejected the idea that Teilhard had any real competence in theology. When discussing the problem of specialisms for the Church, Rahner remarks that a specialist really knows nothing of fields outside his own. He sees Teilhard as a particular illustration of this point: for though a priest and a very good palaeontologist, he was none the less a layman in the field of real theology and philosophy, albeit he did not admit or recognise this fact. Rahner does not regard this judgment as in any way controverted by the fact that Teilhard was a Jesuit priest who had had years of intensive theological training in the seminary in theology as well as philosophy. He sees Teilhard as falling between two stools: theologians think of him as a scientist, but to scientists he is primarily a theologian.[2] Perhaps the real trouble here lies in the definition of theology. Certainly Teilhard does not theologise in a narrowly specialist or technical manner; but theology can be prosecuted in more than one way. He takes

---

[1] *Honest to God*, pp. 114 f.

[2] K. Rahner, 'Zum heutigen Pluralismus in der geistigen Situation der Katholiken und der Kirche', *Stimmen der Zeit*, 176 (June, 1965), pp. 191–199. This opinion is cited by L. Roberts, *The Achievement of Karl Rahner* (Herder, 1967), p. 273 and endorsed by him at p. 160: 'Rahner's views closely resemble those of Teilhard de Chardin, but they are theologically and philosophically subtler and more sophisticated. . . .'

catholic theology for granted and seeks to build upon that foundation, even though he is not uncritical of its traditional formulations, especially where they conflict with the modern view of the world. My own view is that the scientists are more justified in their opinion of Teilhard as primarily a theologian, than Rahner is in his assessment.

The justification of this statement must lie in the answer to our second question, 'how can we classify Teilhard's theology?' Professor John Macquarrie regards his work as belonging to the school of Realist Metaphysical Theology.[1] The term 'Realist' might be confusing here, as it reminds us of the medieval controversy between the realists and the nominalists. However, if we wish to understand Macquarrie's classification, we must explicitly exclude that particular connotation for the term 'realist' here. Macquarrie gives us three criteria for understanding what he means by the name, 'Realist Metaphysics': (1) Realist Metaphysics represents a reaction against philosophical Idealism because it takes science as its starting-point for the apprehension of reality, rather than an *a priori* philosophical belief in the primacy of Mind. (2) Realist Metaphysics does not regard Mind as the essential component of Reality, as Idealism does, and so this type of thought regards the world in time and space as possessing its own reality in its own right. The world's reality is in no way impaired by any lack of cognition of it. Realist Metaphysics would reject the idealist view that the immensities of time and space in the universe are irrelevant or without significance since no consciousness has traversed them. (3) Realist Metaphysics tends towards the view that matter is not hostile to spirit, but rather is inter-penetrated through and through by spirit.

How far does Teilhard's work fulfil these canons? He certainly meets the first criterion: always his point of departure is 'the phenomenal point of view to which I systematically confine myself'.[2] He is certainly in reaction against

---

[1] J. Macquarrie, *Twentieth Century Religious Thought* (S.C.M., 1963), p. 269–273.
[2] *The Phenomenon of Man*, p. 308.

Idealism: as early as 1919 he wrote in a letter, 'While reaching a more precise definition of my points of contact with my friends, I have also come to realise the turn of my mind that divides me from them. I'm less concerned than they are with the metaphysical side of things, with what might have been or might not have been, with the abstractions of existence: all that seems to me inevitably misleading or shaky. I realise that, to the very marrow of my bones, I'm sensitive to the real, to what is made of it. My concern is to discover the conditions for such progress as is open to us, and not, starting from first principles, some theoretical development of the universe. This bias means that I'll always be a philistine to the professional philosophers. . . .'[1] Once more, we can say that he fulfils the third criterion. Of all thinkers who display pan-psychism, i.e. the belief that spirit is an essential constituent of matter and so in no way hostile or alien to matter, none exceeds Teilhard in expounding it: 'Without doubt *there is something* through which material and spiritual energy hold together and are complementary . . . the two energies of mind and matter . . . are constantly associated and in some way pass into each other.'[2] In a superb piece of creative and artistic writing, entitled 'The Spiritual Power of Matter', Teilhard uses as a model, the story of the translation of Elijah into heaven (2 Kings 2), as an occasion for the composition of a Hymn to Matter which is put into the mouth of Elijah as he ascends into heaven: 'I bless you matter, and you I acclaim: not as the pontiffs of science or the moralising preachers depict you, debased, disfigured – a mass of brute force and base appetites – but as you reveal yourself to me today *in your totality and your true nature*. . . .'

'I acclaim you as the universal power which brings together and unites, through which the multitudinous monads are bound together and in which all converge on the way of the spirit.'

[1] *The Making of a Mind*, p. 302. This honest opinion about himself helps us to understand Karl Rahner's judgment on Teilhard as a theologian.
[2] *The Phenomenon of Man*, p. 63 f.

'I acclaim you as the melodious fountain of water whence spring the souls of men and as the limpid crystal whereof is fashioned the new Jerusalem. . . .'

'Your realm comprises those serene heights where saints think to avoid you – but where your flesh is so transparent and so agile as to be no longer distinguishable from spirit.'[1] Teilhard concludes this meditation with a short sentence of surpassing power and dramatic force:

'Down below on the desert sands, now tranquil again, someone was weeping and calling out "My Father, my Father! What wild wind can this be that has borne him away?"'

'And on the ground there lay a cloak.'

It may also be remarked that the editor's apologetic note is pure bathos in its desperate anxiety to 'justify' Teilhard's originality and render it innocuous! Certainly this kind of pan-psychism runs clean counter to the Greek philosophical tradition of Plato and Aristotle in which Roman Catholic thought is so deeply steeped.

Teilhard fulfils the first and third criteria of Macquarrie's classification, but what about the second? The point about the second criterion for Realist Metaphysics is that it shows that this type of thought is a form of philosophical pluralism. It will not allow that Mind is the only constituent reality beside which all other phenomena are secondary or upon which they are dependent. Now I do not think that Teilhard fulfils this second criterion. A superficial view of his approach might suggest that he does and apparently Macquarrie thinks he does; yet when we judge Teilhard's point of view not merely from *The Phenomenon of Man*, but also take into account his other published writings, we begin to see that really the whole of his work comprises a massive christology. We may freely admit that it is a very unusual christology in that it is worked out often in scientific terms, and again in mystical terms, or literary terms, but none the less, for Teilhard, in essence there is no pluralism at the heart of

[1] This meditation is published in *Hymn of the Universe* (Collins, 1965), pp. 68–71.

reality. There is a fundamental unity. This does not mean
that he is an Idealist, because whilst the concept of Mind is
obviously important for Teilhard, as the concept of the
noosphere implies, yet it is not really determinative for his
thought. What does determine his thinking is his faith in
Christ. Christ is the whole of reality as we know it. His
testament of faith is expounded in quite lyrical and poetic
terms in the essay 'Science and Christ' which gives its title
to the book: 'And then comes the question of Christ himself
– who is he? Turn to the most weighty and most unmistak-
able passages in the Scriptures. Question the Church about
her essential beliefs; and this is what you will learn: Christ
is not something added to the world as an extra, he is not
an embellishment, a king as we now crown kings, the owner
of a great estate. . . . He is the alpha and the omega, the
principle and the end, the foundation stone and the key-
stone, the Plenitude and the Plenifier. He is the one who
consummates all things and gives them their consistence. It
is towards him and through him, the inner life and light of
the world, that the universal convergence of all created spirit
is effected in sweat and tears. He is the single centre, precious
and consistent, who glitters at the summit that is to crown
the world, at the opposite pole from those dim and eternally
shrinking regions into which our science ventures when it
descends the road of matter and the past.'[1] Here lies the
heart of Teilhard's approach to Reality, and it affords an
explanation of why his work is so difficult to categorise.
Scientists intuit that Teilhard does not share their passion
for scientific enquiry as an end in itself. Thus M. J. S.
Rudwick, in a review of *The Vision of the Past*, can speak of
Teilhard's 'thinly veiled disdain for the more mundane vision
of "mere scientists" '.[2] However, science, for Teilhard, is
indispensable for affording a view of what God is doing in
his world. It teaches us by its inability to disclose reality
through its analytical method, that reality must be found 'in
the direction in which things become complex in unity, for

[1] *Science and Christ*, pp. 34 f.
[2] This review is published in *Theology*, lxx, 563, p. 232.

in that direction there must lie a supreme centre of convergence and consistence, in which everything is knit together
and holds together. We should be overcome with joy (which
is not putting it too strongly) to note how admirably Jesus
Christ . . . fills this empty place which has been distinguished
by the expectation of all Nature'.[1] Teilhard can testify: 'I
am convinced that there is no more substantial nourishment
for the religious life than contact with scientific realities, if
they are properly understood';[2] and again, 'By itself science
cannot discover Christ – but Christ satisfies the yearnings
that are born in our hearts in the school of science. The cycle
that sends man down to the bowels of matter in its full
multiplicity, thence to climb back to the centre of spiritual
unification is a natural cycle. We could say that it is a divine
cycle, since it was first followed by him who had to "descend
into hell" before ascending into heaven . . . only that man
can fully appreciate the richness contained in the apex of
the cone, who has first gauged the width and power of the
base.'[3] So we may summarise this stage of the discussion by
saying that Teilhard's work fits with difficulty into Macquarrie's classification of 'Realist Metaphysics'; perhaps,
more accurately, it could be termed, 'Realist Christology', as
this alteration would indicate that his work is more monistic
than pluralist in tendency.

It is the disclosure of just how fundamental christology is
to Teilhard's system of thought that makes his comparison
with Dietrich Bonhoeffer and Paul Tillich so appropriate, as
for both these German Protestant theologians christology
also held a crucial place. Both men commend themselves
for this comparison by real affinities of thought with Teilhard
and by their instructive differences of emphasis. Both these
theologians were appreciably critical of each other. Bonhoeffer, in his attack on religion for refusing to accept the
world in its own reality, can say of Tillich: he 'set out to
interpret the evolution of the world itself – against its will –

[1] *Science and Christ*, p. 34.
[2] *Ibid.*, p. 36.
[3] *Ibid.*,

in a religious sense . . . the world unseated him and went
on by itself: he too sought to understand the world better
than it understood itself, but it felt entirely *mis*understood
and rejected the imputation.'[1] Similarly Tillich could question Bonhoeffer: 'Everyone is always quoting *Letters and
Papers from Prison*. Bonhoeffer's martyrdom has given him
authority – martyrdom always gives psychological authority
– but in fact he didn't live long enough for us to know
what he thought.'[2] Despite their differences, Tillich and
Bonhoeffer seem to distil the genius of German Protestant
theology. Bonhoeffer, always open to the best of Barth's
thought, and Tillich, who had absorbed the best of Bultmann,
and then gone on his own way, together they provide an
effective theological focus on the work of Teilhard de
Chardin. Certainly their German theological idiom differs
strikingly from the more literary, lyrical, and intensely individual language and style of Teilhard, but all three share
common concerns. As far as we know, neither Bonhoeffer nor
Teilhard knew anything of each other's work; and so the
interest here lies in how they reached such similar christological convictions without such cross-fertilisation of thought.
Tillich did read *The Phenomenon of Man* and welcomed the
endorsement by so distinguished a theologian-scientist of his
own effort to provide a theological assessment of the knowledge of nature which science has afforded, in the third
volume of his *Systematic Theology*.[3] We now turn to the comparison of Teilhard's christology with that of Bonhoeffer by
first outlining Bonhoeffer's ideas.

2

A great problem for the modern world, and therefore, also
for theology, is the rate of change in the world today. The
accelerating tempo of change threatens us with extreme

[1] Dietrich Bonhoeffer, *Letters and Papers from Prison* (Fontana,
1959), pp. 108 f.
[2] This opinion is cited by Ved Mehta, *The New Theologian* (Pelican,
1968), p. 146.
[3] Paul Tillich, *Perspectives on Nineteenth and Twentieth Century
Theology* (S.C.M., 1967), p. 126.

relativism in all fields of knowledge and experience; old authorities lose their cogency and status, by appearing manifestly dated and so increasingly irrelevant. The schoolboy's question, 'How can a person who lived nearly two thousand years ago be of vital importance for me today?' cannot be airily dismissed as naïveté. Bonhoeffer was peculiarly sensitive to this challenge of faith. He felt the pressure of this question continually. He rephrased it thus: 'The thing that keeps coming back to me is what *is* Christianity, and indeed what *is* Christ, for us today?'[1] Bonhoeffer offered a first response to this question in a series of lectures given at the University of Berlin in the summer semester of 1933, now available in the form of reconstructed students' notes, and published under the simple title of *Christology*.[2] Only the first two sections of the lecture course were delivered; these were entitled, 'The Present Christ' and 'The Historical Christ'. The projected third part was to be concerned with the Eternal Christ, but the pressure of political events in Germany in that year fore-closed the semester. It is Bonhoeffer's exposition of the ever-present Christ which brings out his close affinities to Teilhard's thought about Christ.

Christology, says Bonhoeffer, is really *Logo*logy, as Christ is essentially God's word to us. Man, however, has his own logos or reason and his scientific investigation of the world is an attempt to reduce the multiplicity of phenomena to some sort of order through the light of his logos. His wholehearted commitment to the scientific method involves him in peculiar difficulty when he encounters Christ. For the Logos of God cannot be comprehended by merely human logos. So incompatible is the meaning of Jesus Christ as Logos with man's own logos, that to man, Christ must appear as anti-logos or counter-logos; that is, as irrational. The traditional way in

---

[1] *Letters and Papers from Prison*, p. 91. Teilhard asks this question too, in his essay 'Science and Christ': 'And then comes the question of Christ himself – who is he?', in the book of that name, p. 34.

[2] Dietrich Bonhoeffer, *Christology*, with an introduction by Edwin H. Robertson and translated by John Bowden (Collins, 1966).

which we try to discover the significance of others for us, such as Socrates or Goethe, is quite inapplicable to Christ. Such a method is foredoomed to failure. In typical German fashion, Bonhoeffer works out the antinomy in question-form. The basic scientific question is 'How?', and this basic question prompts a whole string of enquiries designed to elicit sufficient information on the relevant subject to permit a classification; for the classification of data is a basic function of man's logos; but herein lies the peculiar difficulty of Christ: he cannot be classified or categorised, simply because, as Logos of God, he is transcendent to man. All that man can do is to listen to the implicit question that Christ poses to every man, 'Who are you?', and answer in humble penitence and faith. If man questions at all, the question must be phrased in such a way that it does not try to pre-condition God to merely human ideas; so 'How?' is always ruled out as impertinent and unanswerable, in that finitude cannot comprehend infinity. The proper question is 'Who?', which, when asked in humility and faith, can lead on to the sort of disclosure of the divine meaning of Jesus such as we have in St Peter's confession at Caesarea Philippi (Matt. 16:13–20).

'Who?' rather than 'How?' discloses itself as the right question when we consider the relation of the person of Christ to his work. A famous theological riddle is to ask which is more important? Is Jesus regarded as Christ and Lord, because of his work? Or is it because he is who he is, that we recognise his work as for us men and for our salvation? Some Christians would regard this antithesis as unreal and these questions as of necessity complementary rather than opposed: as is the person, so is the work; as is the work, so is the person.[1] Following Luther, though, Bonhoeffer

---

[1] Cf. *Honest to God*, p. 77: 'To say that in him [Jesus], man was completely united with the Ground of his being is to say that on this understanding there is no final difference between the person of Christ and the work of Christ, the incarnation and the at-one-ment. . . .' This use of the vocabulary of Tillich reminds us of his discussion of this problem, in which he differs from Bonhoeffer very strikingly in abandoning the distinction as wholly artificial: cf. Paul Tillich, *Systematic Theology* combined volume (James Nisbet, 1968), Volume II, pp. 194 f.

roundly asserts that we can discover the true nature of Christ's saving work only through a prior grasp of the dignity of his person. We cannot discover the dignity of the person through the work, for each aspect of the work which might suggest his divinity is open to an alternative humanist explanation. Lutherans see here an example of the cardinal principle of justification by faith in operation: Jesus can never be Son of God by virtue of his achievement on the cross, for that would imply that the work was done apart from God; but the real truth is that God was in Christ reconciling the world unto himself (2 Cor. 5:19). The incognito of the incarnation is consistent with the mystery of the divine:

'Truly, thou art a God who hidest thyself,
O God of Israel, the Saviour' (Isa. 45:15).

A seemingly meritorious work can never be free from ambiguity; it may after all be a work of the devil posing as an angel of light. Only a prior knowledge of the person, therefore, can determine the character of the work; so only a prior knowledge of the Christ enables men to see the cross as for our salvation. Saul of Tarsus was quite convinced that the cross proved Jesus to be an impostor and criminal, until he asked the question, 'Tell me, Lord, who are you?' It was when he discovered that the Lord was none other than Jesus 'whom you are persecuting', that he came to see the cross as the power of God unto salvation (Acts 9:1–6).

Bonhoeffer sees christology as consisting of two basic statements: (a) Jesus is the Christ present as the crucified and risen one, and (b) Christ is present in the church as a person. The resurrection is the necessary presupposition of the whole of the first part of the *Christology*, as it alone makes possible the thesis that Christ is the ever-present one. A mere historical Christ, as Luther said, is actually far from us. Only a resurrected and ascended Christ can be truly present to us. The presence of Christ is mediated to us in three ways: as Word, as Sacrament and as Community.

Christ as Word

A difficulty remains to be resolved here. If Christ is the Logos of God, surely then he is always bound to be incomprehensible to man's logos, no matter what question man may ask. Of course, if we interpret the Logos of God as the *mind* of God, this conclusion naturally follows. Bonhoeffer resolves the dilemma by stressing the *word* connotation of logos: God speaks and takes care that man can understand. The Logos of God is God's *address* to man; his address to man is none other than Christ himself. Christ as address implies a relationship between speaker and hearer, so we may say that Christ as Word is God's address through the proclamation of the redeemed community to man and for man. This means that man is always in relationship with God. The implications of this truth are momentous; Christ is not Logos because he is the bearer of timeless truths about God, or else his mission would be more important than his person. It is the person of Christ which is the word of God. Who he is cannot be regarded as less important than what he said, as there is an absolute identity between person and word. It also follows that Christ is encounter: in Christ, God encounters man and man encounters God, and that encounter takes place within each personal space and time of the lives of those encountered by God in Christ. In the concrete moment of personal lives, God in Christ addresses his word of command and forgiveness to man. The mode of his presence in church is as *preaching*. In the foolishness of preaching, as the word of the church, the crucified, resurrected and ascended Lord confronts man.

Christ as Sacrament

Once more we must not ask the wrong question, 'How is Christ present in the sacrament?', as the various answers to this form of the question could serve as a history of Christian division. The disunity occasioned by the different answers to the wrong question about the sacrament is attributable to all the theological solutions from transubstantiation, or consubstantiation and its attendant explanations of what is technically known as ubiquitarianism and ubivoluntarianism, or the Calvinist solution of the extra-corporeality of the Logos during the sacrament, to the Zwinglian solution of the sacrament as nothing but pure symbolism. The dismissal of the sacrament as nothing more than a pious remembrance of the suffering love of the redeeming Lord fails equally as an attempt to answer the wrong question 'how?', as does the doctrine of the sacrifice of the mass. Away with explanations of the miracle of the divine grace! However, once the correct question is asked, 'Who is present in the sacrament?' then, the universal testimony of all Christians unites in proclaiming 'the historical Jesus who was crucified, who is risen and ascended to heaven, the God-man revealed as brother and Lord, as creature and as creator'.[1] Such an answer is an implicit judgment upon all eucharistic theologies affected by the polemics of Christian disunity. If the churches take seriously the crucial truth of the sacrament as Christ present as sacrament for us, and this, surely, is its christological significance, then they must reject any answer which implicitly denies that presence. To regard the sacrament as a *memorial* or *symbol* or as *representative* of Christ is theologically a mistake, as all these words imply that Christ is absent, which is the one thing that he is not!

Christ Present as Community

In the first place this phrase implies the community of the church. There is no discord between the individual and the corporate presence of Christ as Bonhoeffer can say, 'Christ is the community by virtue of his being *pro me*.'[2] Community is the form of Christ for the period between the ascension and the parousia. The church is the word which Christ speaks, and the church exists only as long as Christ continues to speak the church. The importance of the community is that it demonstrates that Christ is not just *spiritually* present: Christ is physically present in space and time as and in community in so far as the church is the body of Christ.

[1] Cf. *Christology*, p. 59.
[2] *Ibid.*

Once more the verb 'to be' has its full existential force; Christ is not merely *represented* by his church. The church *is* the body of Christ. Again, Christ is not just the head of the church; he *is* the community in his whole person. When critics of the church point to those features of her life which appear to deny the truth of such a theological affirmation about her, they are merely pointing out the marks of the humiliation of Christ. From *within* the Church, however, there are equally marks of Christ in his exaltation.

Persons do not exist *in vacuo*; they have a context, and so it is appropriate to ask not merely, 'Who is Christ?' but also 'where is Christ?' This second question is clearly correctly framed because it yields such productive answers. Bonhoeffer discerns three main answers: Christ stands at the centre of nature, at the centre of human existence and of history. A preliminary difficulty commonly felt is that if Christ is so central to the life of man, why is it that he is so irrelevant to modern consciousness. Bonhoeffer fully acknowledges this irrelevance by his formulation that when we first discover Christ he appears on the boundary of our existence: 'In the fallen world, the centre is at the same time the boundary. Man stands between the law and fulfilment. . . . Christ as centre means he is the fulfilment of the law. So he is in turn the boundary and the judgment of man, but at the same time the beginning of his new existence, its centre.'[1] The statement about Christ as the centre is described as 'not psychological but ontological-theological'.

Christ as the Centre of History

Such a statement can never be proved as it is an assertion of faith. History, which is a relative, can never give rise to a deduction of an absolute character. But in so far as history has an interim character in that it stands between promise and fulfilment, the meaning of history is found in the appearance of a messiah. The history of the world is littered with appearances of false messiahs; however, in and through Israel the true messiah appears, who is the crown of history's

[1] *Christology*, pp. 62 f.

perennial expectation and the judgment of history's false hopes, occasioned by its floundering attempts to realise its intrinsic and ineradicable yearning for messianic fulfilment. The only form of the messiah that history can know is that of a crucified messiah. Here, Bonhoeffer doubtless alludes to the different character of the events of the Cross and Resurrection, so well formulated by Tillich: 'But there is a qualitative difference. While the stories of the Cross probably point to an event that took place in the full light of historical observation, the stories of the Resurrection spread a veil of deep mystery over the event.'[1] Bonhoeffer asserts history as the dimension of the cross as eternity is the dimension of the resurrection. In so far as Christ is the fulfilment of the messianic hope, he becomes the centre of history. It follows from what was said above about Christ present as community, that the Christ, who is present as church at the centre of history, makes the church the centre of the state. Of course Bonhoeffer is not thinking of established churches like the Church of England, but is drawing out in general terms the theological implications of the church for the state, and he does so by using exactly the same categories for this relationship as he did for describing the centrality of Christ for human existence: boundary and centre, promise and fulfilment again feature. The church is both the boundary and the centre of the state in so far as history comprises the life of the state; the church is the boundary of the state, when the state comes under the judgment of the cross; but the church is the fulfilment of the state and thus its centre in so far as the church is Christ present as community. Bonhoeffer writes: 'As long as Christ was on earth he was the rule of God. When he was crucified, the rule broke into two, one by his right hand and one by the left hand of God. Now his rule can be known only as two-fold; as church and as state. But the whole Christ is present to his church and this church is the hidden centre of the state, but in fact it lives from this centre and cannot continue without it.'[2]

[1] *Systematic Theology*, Vol. II, p. 177.
[2] *Christology*, p. 66.

Christ as the Centre of Nature

Bonhoeffer confesses the failure of Protestantism in the past to give this topic adequate consideration.[1] Doubtless the failure is due to the bias against Natural Theology and the emphasis on Revelation alone as the medium of true knowledge of God which are characteristic of the Lutheran tradition. However, Bonhoeffer sees Christ as the centre of nature in his role as the mediator. Christ knows what creaturehood is all about because he is *the* new Creature. As such he is the judgment of alienated creation. Before the Fall, creation was truly a word of God, but now by reason of the fact that it is a fallen creation, it has lost the capacity to proclaim God's word: 'It is now dumb, in thrall under the guilt of men'.[2] This is perhaps rather a gloomy and pessimistic view and certainly discounts the glad rejoicing in nature as the trumpet of God in his glory and majesty, which is so characteristic of the Old Testament.[3] For the prophet Hosea, for example, the beauty of nature is a type of the blessedness of life reconciled to God.[4] Bonhoeffer here demonstrates the paucity of the tradition to which he is heir. His mind is directed towards natural catastrophes in nature, which he sees as really the blind, lumbering movements of nature as she seeks her ideal freedom which she cannot achieve by her own efforts. Nature needs not merely liberation, but redemption. In so far as Christ is the centre of nature, he is the guarantee that nature has been truly redeemed; the decisive work has been performed; and though secure in principle, it has not yet been realised in fact. Here Bonhoeffer's thought is very much guided by the apostolic discussion in Romans 8: 19–23:

'For the creation waits with eager longing for the revealing of the sons of God; for the creation was subjected to futility, not of its own will but by the will of him who

---

[1] Cf. his discussion in D. Bonhoeffer, *Ethics* (Fontana, 1964), pp. 143–155.

[2] *Christology*, p. 66.

[3] Cf. Ps. 19:1–6.

[4] Cf. Hosea 14:5–7.

subjected it in hope; because the creation itself will be set free from its bondage to decay and obtain the glorious liberty of the children of God. We know that the whole creation has been groaning in travail together until now. . . .'

The situation of waiting means that the creation is redeemed in hope. The consecration of the bread and wine in the Eucharist is a kind of first-fruits or anticipation of nature's coming freedom: 'the enslaved old creation is made free for its new freedom'.[1] Enslaved nature is unable to utter God's word, but the sacrament proclaims the word of God because it proclaims the presence of Christ; for in the sacrament, nature has been liberated by Christ to reveal Christ as the centre of nature. Bonhoeffer concludes the first part of his deeply stimulating *Christology* with the remark that in so far as man is a part of nature, what Christ does for man, he does for nature:

'As fulfiller of the law and liberator of creation, the mediator acts for the whole of human existence. He is the same, who is intercessor and *pro me*, and who is himself the end of the old world and the beginning of the new world of God.'[2]

It is at this point that we first see how these two men, Teilhard and Bonhoeffer, meet on common ground, though their routes to this common point are so different. However, Bonhoeffer is best known today for his famous *Letters and Papers from Prison* and to complete the comparison we must first ask whether these letters add anything to his concept of the centrality of Christ. We may recall that Teilhard was also a great letter writer and his letters are as much evidence for his thought as his later, more polished works.

In the letters of Bonhoeffer we have passages where he works out tentatively the radical implications of the centrality of Christ for Christian strategy in the modern world. God

[1] *Christology*, p. 67.
[2] *Ibid.*

must be found in the heart of knowledge: in the letter dated 25 May, 1944, Bonhoeffer comments on von Weizsäcker's book on the world view of physics: 'It has brought home to me how wrong it is to use God as a stop-gap for the incompleteness of our knowledge. For the frontiers of knowledge are inevitably being pushed back further and further, which means that you only think of God as a stop-gap. He also is being pushed back farther and farther and is in more or less continuous retreat. We should find God in what we do know, not in what we don't; not in outstanding problems, but in those we have already solved. This is true not only for the relation between Christianity and science, but also for the wider human problems such as guilt, suffering and death. . . . Once more God cannot be used as a stop-gap. We must not wait until we are at the end of our tether: he must be found at the centre of life: in life and not only in death; in health and vigour, and not only in suffering; in activity, and not only in sin. The ground for this lies in the revelation of God in Christ. Christ is the centre of life. . . . In Christ there are no Christian problems.'[1] A month later he was attacking the misconceived apologetic of 'futile rear-guard actions against Darwinism, etc.', which he saw as arising from the attempt to cope with the effect of Kantian philosophy which had removed God to the realm beyond experience. Bonhoeffer wanted to bring God firmly back into the centre again. He censures the out-moded mission tactics of the church which try to bring men to the end of their tether before they are regarded as ready for the ministrations of the church. This view, once more, depends upon a God who is a kind of *deus ex machina*, essentially a problem-solver and who, in the unbelief of the church, is not seen as having anything to give man in his health and strength.[2] In another letter, dated 27 June, 1944, Bonhoeffer rejects the idea that the Christian hope for the future is eternal bliss. The purpose of the resurrection is not to give hope beyond the grave, but rather it 'sends a man back to his life on earth in a wholly

[1] *Letters and Papers from Prison*, p. 104.
[2] *Ibid.*, pp. 114 f.

new way'.[1] In the same letter Bonhoeffer concludes that the chief characteristic of salvation myths is that they arise from human experiences of the boundary situation. By this expression he means not only death, but all those crises where the frailty and helplessness of man are starkly evident. Christ is not merely the Christ of the last rites, rather, 'Christ takes hold of a man at the centre of his life'.[2]

It was the demand that Christ should be seen as the centre of human existence which provoked the insight that Christ should be thought of as encountering man not in weakness, but in his strength; not in some hidden, interior, vulnerable privacy, but in his public, confident life: 'This is why I am so anxious that God should not be relegated to some last secret place, but that we should frankly recognise that the world and men have come of age, that we should not speak ill of man in his worldliness, but confront him with God at his strongest point, that we should give up all our clerical subterfuges, and our regarding of psychotherapy and existentialism as precursors of God. . . .'[3]

The theme of man's adulthood is, therefore, a new way of demanding that Christ should be made truly central to the modern world, because it is a demand that Christ should be seen to be relevant to the modern world's needs. Such relevance can never be demonstrated when the church insists on treating the world as spiritually juvenile, and totally ignorant of spiritual matters. In past ages when man was genuinely adolescent and under tutelage, then God as omnipotent problem-solver, exercising a benevolent patronage, was extremely relevant; but now that man is genuinely adult, Bonhoeffer has the intuition that it is the presentation of God to man in the weakness and powerlessness of the cross that will be most relevant.[4]

How does this outline of Bonhoeffer's christology compare with Teilhard's? In a perceptive article in *Theology*,[5] entitled 'The Future of Man', Professor D. M. Mackinnon refers to

[1] *Letters and Papers from Prison*, p. 112.   [2] *Ibid.*, p. 113.
[3] *Ibid.*, p. 118.   [4] *Ibid.*, pp. 106, 120–124, 125–127.
[5] *Theology*, lxxii, 586, p. 152.

Professor Heinrich Ott's book, *Wirklichkeit und Glaube* in the first volume of which he compares the christologies of Bonhoeffer and Teilhard. Mackinnon comments: 'For both men, vastly different though their formation and experience were, at the centre of their faith lay an overwhelming sense of the presence of *God-in-Christ* in the ordinary ways of the world; according to Ott (and I do not quite agree with him here) Teilhard learned this lesson in the deserts of Central Asia, when engaged in palaeontological research, while Bonhoeffer made this vision his own in the prison cell in which he spent the last years of his life before his own execution.' Mackinnon records Ott's conclusion that Teilhard's christology is that of the Christ of Easter Day, whilst Bonhoeffer's is the Christ of Good Friday. But is this judgment really true? The distinction between Teilhard and Bonhoeffer just cited is an exaggeration which seems to have been produced through insufficient acquaintance with the whole range of both men's writings. It takes virtually no account of Bonhoeffer's *Christology* of 1933 and relies too heavily on the impression made by the christology of the *Letters and Papers from Prison*. What such generalisations often fail to account for is the influence of context on theological composition. It is wholly natural and appropriate that a man writing in prison should see the powerful relevance of the crucified Christ, and there is no doubt that Bonhoeffer's imprisonment afforded him real insight into the meaning of the Christ of Good Friday. Yet Bonhoeffer's sense of the ever-present Christ can hardly be confined to the time spent in prison. It is, as we have seen, the explicit theme of the first section of the *Christology* lectures, and it is interesting to repeat the grounds Bonhoeffer found for his statement of Christ as ever-present: 'To begin christology with this statement of one who is present, has the advantage that Jesus is understood from the start as the Risen One who has ascended into heaven.'[1]

Similarly, whilst it is undeniable that the resurrection is

[1] *Christology*, p. 49.

quite cardinal for Teilhard, yet when he is writing after a battle during the First World War, it is quite natural that it is the Christ of Good Friday who occupies his thoughts: 'I don't know what sort of monument the country will later put up on Froideterre hill to commemorate the great battle. There's only one that would be appropriate: a great figure of Christ. Only the image of the crucified can sum up, express and relieve all the horror, and beauty, all the hope and deep mystery in such an avalanche of conflict and sorrows.'[1] Context, while it may deeply influence the form in which theology is expressed, however, does not determine it. It was Bonhoeffer's meditation on the Christ of Good Friday that made the Christ of Easter Day no less real to him even in prison. In the *Letters and Papers from Prison*, he makes the following points: men fear dying, far more than death. The New Testament, however, proclaims victory over death and this, of course, is guaranteed by the resurrection: 'We need not *ars moriendi*, the art of dying, but the resurrection of Christ to invigorate and cleanse the world today. . . . To live in the light of the resurrection – that is the meaning of Easter.'[2] When Bonhoeffer is arguing for the centrality of Christ for modern life, once more it is the resurrection which occurs to him as one of the powerful arguments for the reform of missionary strategy for which he pleads: 'Belief in the resurrection is not the solution of the problem of death,'[3] for 'the difference between the Christian hope of resurrection and a mythological hope is that the Christian hope sends a man back to his life on earth in a wholly new way. . . . The Christian . . . like Christ himself ("My God, my God, why hast thou forsaken me?") must drink the earthly cup to the lees, and only in so doing is the crucified and risen Lord with him and he crucified and risen with Christ.'[4]

This last quotation gives us the true perspective on Bonhoeffer's christology; for him it is wholly false and even

[1] *The Making of a Mind*, p. 119.
[2] *Letters and Papers from Prison*, p. 85.
[3] *Ibid.*, p. 93.
[4] *Ibid.*, p. 112.

distorting to distinguish between the cross and resurrection – together they constitute the unique significance of the ever-present Christ. In fact the real problem for Bonhoeffer in prison was not to relate the resurrection to the need for placing Christ at the centre of the life of man – that application was all too obvious and he was never guilty of labouring the obvious. The real problem that faced him was to show the relevance of the cross to man in his strength and confident life. It had always been easy to see the relevance of the cross to the problem of the evil and suffering in the world, but that was precisely the sort of boundary situation in human affairs on which the Church had always concentrated, and which Bonhoeffer, in prison, felt was a profound mistake for the missionary strategy of the Church. His startling message in the *Letters* is the suggestion that if the Church really wants to win the modern world for Christ, then the world at its strongest and best, at its least need of God because of the excellence of its science and understanding, is the world to which God in the weakness and powerlessness of the Cross must be presented, and it will be only the grace of God and the power of the resurrection which will enable the church to live this diminishment, sacrifice all its advantages, give away all its wealth, and live a truly crucified life before a godless, powerful world.

If the Christ of Easter Day is the note which seems to predominate in Teilhard's christology, once more it is a deceptive antithesis. Professor Mackinnon is fully justified in dissenting from Ott's opinion that Teilhard developed his faith in the ever-present Christ in the deserts of China. Long before his first visit to China, while he was still a stretcher-bearer in the First World War, he wrote an essay, 'The Mystical Milieu'.[1] Beginning with a meditation on the consecrated bread of the sacrament, Teilhard develops its meaning:

'You came down into me by means of a tiny scrap of created reality; and then, suddenly, you unfurled your

[1] This essay is published in *Writings in Time of War* (Collins, 1968), pp. 117–149.

immensity before my eyes and displayed yourself to me as Universal Being.'[1] In this new light he begins to understand death and the order of privation and diminishment:

'I know, Lord, that you will send me . . . deprivations, sorrow. The object of my love will fall away from me, or I shall outgrow it. The flower I held in my hands withered in my hands. At the turn of the lane a wall rose up before me. . . . A flame burnt up the paper on which my thought was written. . . .'[2]; but in the midst of the sorrow he experienced an invasion of unexpected joy, as he found that diminishment led to communion with that inexpressible reality that lay behind all things: 'Soon, however, its autonomy became apparent as a strange and supremely desirable Omnipresence. . . . What name can we give to this mysterious Entity? . . . I can feel it: he has a name and a face, but he alone can reveal his face and pronounce his name: Jesus!'[3] Reflection on the meaning of his own person led Teilhard to realise 'that it was all coming to centre *on a single point*, on a Person: your Person: Jesus! In his superabundant unity, that person possessed the virtue of each one of the lower mystical circles. His presence impregnated and sustained all things. His power animated all energy. His mastering life ate into every other life, to assimilate it to himself.'[4]

This passage highlights the resemblance and the contrast between Teilhard and Bonhoeffer. I am convinced that there is a very real theological identity between them in that they conceived of the ever-present Christ as the crucified and risen Lord, supremely at the centre of all things. The difference is seen particularly in the writing which reflects the differences in temperament and personality. In Bonhoeffer the theology is spelt out in precise, articulated, balanced sentences reflecting the equally precise and careful thought, so typical of German theologians. Bonhoeffer is the man of affairs as well as a theologian and so expresses a theology of the every-day life, of politics, of the on-going daily rush of

[1] *Ibid.*, p. 120.
[2] *Ibid.*, p. 126.   [3] *Ibid.*, p. 145.
[4] *Ibid.*, p. 146.

the great world in history and the relevance of Christ to it. For Teilhard, scientist, mystic, poet and literary artist, Christ is seen and apprehended as much intuitively as intellectually; seen and grasped in context of the evolving universe, in terms of the minutiae of atomic physics, through the six hundred million years of evolving life on this earth, to the unimaginably glorious destiny that awaits creation in the loving purposes of God: 'All around us, Christ is physically active in order to control all things. From the ultimate vibration of the atom to the loftiest mystical contemplation; from the lightest breeze that ruffles the air to the broadest currents of life and thought, he ceaselessly animates, without disturbing, all the earth's processes.'[1] In Bonhoeffer we miss this note of the universal Christ. It would be dangerous to say, though, that it was not there in his thought. It is logically implied in the concept of the ever-present Christ, and it may well have belonged to the third section of his *Christology* which, alas, never saw the light of day. Yet with Teilhard the universal Christ is the very first note to be struck in his christology and it is almost impossible to think of the meaning of Christ for Teilhard without thinking of the cosmic and universal Christ. Also in Bonhoeffer we miss the sense of *genesis*, or *evolution* and *process* which is so fundamental for Teilhard. The biblically orientated thought of Bonhoeffer still reflects in its feel, at any rate, the 'static universe of the theologians', at least as far as Christ himself is concerned, whereas Teilhard is so conscious of the flux of everything that the meaning of reality must be seen in terms of this flux, and this has its due effect on his doctrine of the person of Christ. Christ grows, Christ feeds on us as we do on him, of all the processes in flow in the universe we can say, 'Christ gains physically from everyone of them. Everything that is good in the universe . . . is gathered up by the Incarnate Word as a nourishment that it assimilates, transforms and divinises',[2] on the way to the Pleroma, which can be defined as the maturity of the universe. Once more we hear a chord struck which reminds us of similarity and difference in the

[1] *Science and Christ*, p. 59.   [2] *Ibid.*

thought of these two great men. Bonhoeffer speaks eloquently and impressively of a world *come of age*,[1] and the phrase 'man come of age' has entered the vocabulary of current theology, yet this idea is expressed similarly yet differently in Teilhard as early as 1920:

'A more realistic and more Christian view shows us earth evolving towards a state in which man, having come into the full possession of his sphere of action, his strength, his maturity and his unity, will at last have become an adult being; and having reached this apogee of his responsibility and freedom, holding in his hands all his future and all his past, will make the choice between arrogant autonomy and loving excentration.'[2] Why the difference in the time-scale between their estimate of when it is appropriate to speak of the adulthood of man? Bonhoeffer is thinking of the time-scale of history whereas Teilhard's time-scale is that of evolution. Possibly Bonhoeffer, also, shares unconsciously with so many of us an attitude towards evolution explicitly repudiated by Teilhard, that evolution is just a biological explanation of how man came to be, and so came to an end with the appearance of man; whereas for Teilhard man is still in mid-course of evolution. This difference in world-view has its inevitable effect on christology as indicated.

3

The theme of the cosmic and universal Christ as the possible point of greatest difference between Bonhoeffer and Teilhard is, also, precisely the point of greatest affinity between Teilhard de Chardin and Paul Tillich. Intellectually there were great differences between them. Tillich was a philosopher quite as much as a theologian, extremely systematic and precise in his thinking, of the very widest interests, a real polymath of encyclopaedic range of mind. Philosophically he is distinguished by a carefully articulated doctrine of Being, which has led to some doubts about the orthodoxy of his view of the person of Christ; so much so that, like Teilhard,

[1] Cf. *Letters and Papers from Prison*, pp. 106–110, 114, 118–122.
[2] *The Future of Man*, p. 19.

some have felt it necessary to defend him against misrepresentation and misunderstanding.[1] A. T. Mollegen emphasises the Christocentric character of Tillich's theology: 'his theology is radically Christocentric. He always speaks about art, science, philosophy, history and religion with the purpose of understanding and disclosing their relation to Christ.'[2] Tillich's starting point is man; and he claims that this is the inevitable starting point for men. He believes that human experience raises questions about the nature of reality, and that the divine answer to the questions that man raises is given to us through the Christian religion. His massive *Systematic Theology* discusses five such questions and answers: human rationality is itself a question that receives the answer of divine revelation; the transience of human life, as a perennial question in all cultures, receives the answer of the being of God; the question of sin receives the answer of Christ, the New Being; the question provoked by man's living unity receives the answer of the Holy Spirit; and the problems of human destiny receive their solution in the promise of the kingdom of God. It is problematic man who is impelled by the ambiguity of his own life to the discovery of God. Rudolf Bultmann and Paul Tillich have this in common that they both worked out the theological significance of Martin Heidegger's philosophy. Bultmann was of the opinion that Martin Heidegger's analysis of the human situation, which he called 'the existential analytic' in his book *Being and Time*, was an exact description of the alienation man experiences, as outlined in the New Testament; so for Bultmann, the existentialism of Heidegger provided a modern language and idiom for him to demythologise the mythology of the New Testament. Where Tillich differs from Bultmann is that he provides a new vocabulary for the 'existential analytic' taken from depth-psychology. Whereas

[1] Cf. B. S. Moss in *The New Theologians* (Mowbrays, 1964), p. 35; A. T. Mollegen in *The Theology of Paul Tillich*, edited by Charles W. Kegley and R. W. Bretall (Macmillan, 1964), p. 231. The whole volume, in some sense, can be said to be an apologia for Paul Tillich's theology, though some of the contributions are none the less critical.

[2] *The Theology of Paul Tillich*, p. 230.

Bultmann stopped with the translation of the New Testament view of man into the categories of existential analysis, Paul Tillich, like Martin Heidegger, believes that the existential analysis of the human condition is incomplete by itself; it needs a philosophy of being to make it intelligible. For Tillich the ambiguity of human life is best expressed by calling it 'existence', which, like Heidegger, he proceeds to analyse etymologically. The study of the history of the word gives its basic connotation, 'To stand out'. In trying to cope with the English cultural tradition of nominalism that almost wholly rejects any kind of philosophy of Being, Tillich ingeniously uses as an analogy the word 'outstanding' which provokes questions and observations. Anyone who is out-standing can only be understood as distinctive if we know the generality to which he is outstanding, i.e. among whom he still partially stands, and yet from which he is distinctive. This analogy serves perfectly for the explanation of existence: it has both positive and negative aspects. The positive side is seen in so far as it displays real 'being'; the negative side is the 'potentiality' for being which all relative non-being must have. The Greeks distinguished between absolute non-being οὐκ ὄν, i.e. nothingness, and relative non-being, μὴ ὄν, which is mere potentiality. Because man lives a life of flux from birth to death, he has finite being, i.e. he is a combina-tion of positive and negative aspects, of being and non-being (ὄν + μὴ ὄν). The latter aspect takes the form of estrange-ment from the true life of man. Tillich in one of his sermons on Mary and Martha,[1] expounds the human condition: 'In experiencing life men experience *concern*. What does it mean to be concerned about something? It means we are involved in it . . . that we participate with our hearts. . . . It points to the way in which we are involved, namely *anxiously*. The wisdom of our language often identifies concern with anxiety.' But this anxiety is not neurotic; it is rational and inevitable for anyone who lives responsibly. For all our con-cerns, *viz.* our work, our personal relationships, our self-consciousness, our daily pre-occupations with food, clothing

[1] Paul Tillich, *The New Being* (S.C.M., 1956), p. 153.

and shelter are none the less transitory and finite, because behind all things stands the inevitability of death. A kind of chain reaction sets in: anxiety and finitude make us insecure; insecurity makes men hostile towards themselves, life in general, and towards God. The experience of estrangement from God deprives life of all meaning, and yet because we cannot from our hearts endorse the fact that life is meaningless, we intuit that it must be our fault and so feel guilty. All these different negative elements: anxiety, finitude, transitoriness, insecurity, hostility, estrangement, meaninglessness and guilt, constitute the side of non-being, which is a fundamental ingredient of the life of man. The other side, the positive side, is that despite all these hindrances and discouragements, man, nevertheless, has the power to affirm his existence and to live as if life is supremely worthwhile. This 'courage to be'[1] points to genuine being, and man's partial realisation of true being raises the logical demand for absolute being – which is another name for God, who may then be described as 'the Ground of our Being', in that he is the necessary pre-condition for the existence of everything else that is. God is our ultimate concern: all our lesser concerns and anxieties point to an ultimate concern which assumes overriding priority over all lesser concerns. This ultimate concern, which may become more important than life itself, clearly transcends the concerns of finitude and so truly merits the description of *ultimate*. In this sense there are no atheists, for every man has one concern that takes precedence over all others. It may be an unworthy concern, which is another name for idolatry. How do we know, though, that the logical demand for a fundamental principle as the necessary condition of all other existing entities is, in fact, valid? If all actual lives demonstrated the same ambiguity which is characteristic of all human life, then belief in a Ground of our Being would be a pure act of intellectual faith; however, there has been one life in history, namely Jesus who

---

[1] Tillich made this phrase famous by using it as the title of one of his expositions of the nature of anxiety: *The Courage To Be* (Fontana, 1962).

is the Christ, whose life has demonstrated a new quality of life. Jesus who is the Christ has by the way in which he lived shown forth the New Being, the crown of all the aspirations and the judgment of all the defects of human life. The New Being is the guarantee of the authenticity of faith in God, the Ground of our Being.

Tillich believes that the best way of understanding with a view to identifying true being is to examine human life and in so far as it shows forth true being, by analysis we can pin-point the structure of being. One of the basic questions in any language is the question, 'What is it?' This question reveals the structure of being which is a *subject-object structure*. The subject-object structure is the experience of self-relatedness. Tillich writes: 'A self is not a thing that may or may not exist; it is an original phenomenon which logically precedes all questions of existence. . . . Man is a fully developed and completely centred self. He "possesses" himself in the form of self-consciousness. He has an ego-self.'[1] Man, however, is not alone: 'Man *has* a world, although he is in it at the same time.'[2] By 'world', Tillich does not mean a rag-bag sum of everything that is, but rather the Greek idea of a cosmos, an ordered whole. A current idiom expresses this exactly when we talk of 'the world of Walter Mitty' or, indeed, of anybody else. Of course the world both affects and is affected by the self which is its centre. Here Tillich's thought comes very close to that of Teilhard who also talks of man as a centred structure. There appears to be a real identity of thought at this point. Tillich expands his meaning: 'When man looks at his world, he looks at himself as an infinitely small part of his world. Although he is the perspective-centre, he becomes a particle of what is centred in him, a particle of the universe. This structure enables man to encounter himself. Without its world the self would be an empty form. Self-consciousness would have no content, for every content, psychic as well as bodily, lies within the universe. There is no self-consciousness without world-consciousness, but the converse is also true. World-consciousness

[1] *Systematic Theology*, Vol. I, p. 188.   [2] *Ibid.*, p. 189.

is possible only on the basis of a fully developed self-consciousness. . . . The interdependence of ego-self and world is the basic ontological structure and implies all others.'[1]

So much for the structure of being, but of what does this structure consist? Tillich distinguishes four elements which together constitute this centred structure of the related self: (a) individualisation and participation, (b) dynamics and form, (c) vitality and intention, (d) freedom and destiny. These are *polarities* – that is, opposite forces held together by their very opposition. In being held together they modify each other and help to create that which is not any one of them individually. If these polarities exist in right relationship within themselves and in relationship to each other, they combine to make true being; but in so far as they are manifested in the life of man, they are subject to threat – the threat of non-being, which has the effect of severing the polarities. In so far as man is defined as a combination of ontic and meontic being (or positive and negative, or being and non-being), his experience of these polarities is a dualistic tension: he experiences them at times in their right relationships and this is the source of his power to affirm life; but he also experiences them in their wrong relationships and this is the source of all that is wrong and distorted within human life. When the polarities are severed, then each end of the polarity is out of control, and so assumes a menacing and retrograde effect in the life of man. In the first polarity, individualisation becomes loneliness, isolation and estrangement; whilst participation becomes the denial of all true individuality in the 'mass-man' with ready-made, standardised opinions and tastes; in the second polarity, the effect of non-being is to turn dynamics into chaotic uncontrollable drives, whilst form degenerates into the fixity of hide-bound custom and rigidity. The polarities of vitality and intention are disrupted by non-being into anarchy on the one hand and stifling legalism on the other. In the last polarity, freedom is driven into irresponsibility and irrationality, whilst

[1] *Systematic Theology*, Vol. I, p. 189.

destiny is perverted into inexorable fate that destroys true free-dom. However, the life of Jesus who is the Christ points to the genuine relationship of these polarities in their authentic, dialectical inter-dependence, by the absence of stress and hostility between the polarities:

(*a*) Individualisation and participation – Jesus who is the Christ is truly unique and most individual, who still attracts millions by the arresting quality of his personality, and yet at the same time, he displays his unique individuality by his remarkable ability to participate in the lives, needs, anxieties and aspirations of his fellows. An analogy here may serve: the life and soul of a party is that distinguished individual whose verve and vitality is chiefly displayed in his unique ability to participate unselfconsciously. Jesus is uniquely 'the man for others'.

(*b*) Dynamics and form – The unity of these polarities in Jesus as the Christ is seen in that he is the union of creative power and rational structure. This is the meaning of the formula: 'Jesus is the Logos':[1] 'The Logos reveals the mystery [of God] and reunites the estranged by appearing as a historical reality in a personal life.' What Tillich wishes to say about this polarity is that form supplies the logic of being which releases dynamics from the mere potentiality of being in the union of dynamics and form. Form is what makes a being a definite being. If for a human life the ideal is 'to thine own self be true', then this can never be realised unless form and dynamics exist in perfect harmony. In Jesus who is the Christ there is no fierce inner contradiction, that threatens his identity.

(*c*) Vitality and intention – Jesus who is the Christ reveals the power of the New Being in that as Christ he is the end of the hide-bound, rigid legalism of man's unavailing attempts to propitiate and reconcile God to man; as he reveals that it is God who reconciles alienated, estranged man. The grace and truth of the New Being, however, is not anti-nomianism or spiritual anarchy, but has the interior discipline of love.

[1] *Systematic Theology*, Vol. II, pp. 128 f.

(*d*) Freedom and destiny – these are the true opposites. Traditionally the argument has been posed between freedom and determinism; however, this was always a bad argument for both sides. The defenders of freedom were forced to champion it in the wrong terms because they conceived of free-will as a thing and so had to seize upon such irrelevancies as Heisenberg's Principle of Indeterminacy to provide a kind of built-in guarantee in the heart of the atom of human freedom. Such an argument is a mistake as logically it issues in the conclusion that freedom is identified with irresponsibility, inconsistency and irrationality – as these are precisely the qualities which defy prediction – a necessary point to gain, so it was thought, to prove that man was free. The champion of freedom never wanted to end up by asserting man's essential unpredictability, but was driven to this half-way house by the terms of the argument. However, the argument is equally unsatisfactory for the behaviourist; for if his deterministic argument is valid, then, he cannot help fashioning the argument which he presents, and whether or not his argument is accepted is equally determined, so it is particularly irrational to formulate the argument in the first place, as the premiss of any argument must be that the hearer of it has an essential freedom to decide for or against its validity, purely on the basis of its logical merits. These logical difficulties indicate that determinism is not the true opposite of freedom, but instead we should select destiny as the true opposite. If freedom is a range of genuine options that are really open to choice, then destiny arises from the free decision – i.e. the 'cutting-off'. Tillich explains:

'The self-centred person does the weighing and reacts as a whole, through his personal centre, to the struggle of motives. This reaction is called "decision". The word "decision", like the word "incision" involves the image of cutting. A decision cuts off possibilities, and these were real possibilities; otherwise no cutting would have been necessary.'[1] Destiny, therefore, is no oppressive fate which annihilates freedom, but rather is the fixed result of a series of free choices: 'Destiny

[1] *Systematic Theology*, Vol. I, p. 204.

is not a strange power which determines what shall happen to me. It is myself as given, formed by nature, history and myself. My destiny is the basis of my freedom; my freedom participates in shaping my destiny.'[1] Jesus reveals the New Being, because he realises his destiny as Christ by the free self-sacrifice of everything which is merely 'Jesus' in him, to what is demanded of him as 'the Christ'. His ability to sacrifice Jesus who is Jesus to Jesus who is the Christ reveals his supreme freedom and his transcendent destiny in glorious unity. Jesus as the Christ reveals the nature of God as Being-in-itself or the Ground of our Being. As in him, so in God, the polarities of the ontological structure of being are displayed, not in conflict and tension so characteristic of the human condition, but in mutual inclusiveness and rest. This is so, because in God there is no threat of non-being to disrupt the essential unity of the polar elements of being. Yet for Jesus as the Christ there is subjection to all the limitations of finite existence as for the rest of men. The difference, therefore, between Being-in-itself which is God, and the New Being who is Jesus as the Christ, is that in Jesus we see the essential life lived under the conditions of existence. Existence is here seen as a fall from essence. Christ heals the existential ills of human life, so enabling man to recover his essential life, i.e. the new being.

This uniquely conceived christology has drawn serious criticism from some of the most sympathetic of Tillich's expositors,[2] as it implies that it is possible to separate between the New Being and Jesus. A. J. McKelway writes: 'Tillich means . . . that there is a line of revelatory and saving events which leads up to and proceeds from the centre of revelation and salvation found in Jesus as the Christ. This line is broadened into a universal presence of the saving power of the New Being without which the "self-destructive structure of existence" would plunge "mankind into complete annihilation".[3] If salvation were contingent upon an encounter

[1] *Ibid.*
[2] Cf. A. J. McKelway, *The Systematic Theology of Paul Tillich* (Lutterworth, 1964), pp. 173–188.   [3] *Systematic Theology*, Vol. II, p. 193.

with Jesus as the Christ, then, Tillich argues, only a few men would be saved – an "absurd and demonic idea" which theologies of universalism have tried to avoid. The concept of healing delivers theology from this dilemma. All men are somewhat saved by the power of the New Being, or else they would have no being.'[1] McKelway criticises Tillich because he maintains that there is healing power of the New Being apart from Jesus as the Christ, but in McKelway's view Tillich is not prepared to identify the New Being with Jesus as the Christ, though he is prepared to state the converse that Jesus who is the Christ manifests the New Being. McKelway's criticism focusses on the role of the Christ: 'Tillich's position . . . is this: Jesus is the Christ because his contemporaries recognised in him the manifestation of the divine Logos, the eternal principle of God's self-revelation called the New Being. The Logos or New Being transcends the event of Jesus, the Christ, though it is manifest in him. . . . Tillich maintains that John (in the prologue to the Gospel) not only allows but directs our attention from Jesus to this divine "principle".' But McKelway denies this: 'We find in John no "higher principle", name, or concept than Jesus Christ. The first sentence of the Gospel does not point up and away from Jesus, but down the page and into the story of his life which it contains. . . . The New Testament is consistent in its sharp and clear focussing on the person of Jesus Christ. Its authors did not, and we dare not, look elsewhere, because there is nowhere else to look. . . . In Jesus Christ we see God and for this reason our gaze may not wander'.[2] McKelway believes that the basic fault of Tillich's theology is that it begins with man, whereas it ought to begin with Jesus Christ, the expression of God's humanity. Yet there is a very nice but crucially important point here. In McKelway we have the traditional, biblical, christological point of view that all we can know of God is what we know of Jesus Christ. This is all very well, if this earth is the only planet where there is a society of conscious intelligent beings

---

[1] *The Systematic Theology of Paul Tillich*, p. 173.
[2] *Ibid.*, pp. 177–179.

over against God. The possibility of many other planets with corporeal, intelligent life upon them is taken very seriously by many sober scientists today. Would such beings be involved in the Fall of necessity? If so, or if not, what is their relation to Jesus who is the Christ? It is certainly easier to conceive of a relationship to the New Being, than it is to Jesus as the Christ. I think this is one of the reasons why Tillich drew the distinction that he did, which has raised this serious critique that McKelway expresses so finely. Tillich was certainly aware of the problem: 'In discussing the character of the quest for and the expectation of the Christ, a question arises which has been carefully avoided by many traditional theologians, even though it is . . . alive for most contemporary people. It is the problem of how to understand the meaning of the symbol "Christ" in the light of the immensity of the universe, the heliocentric system of planets, the infinitely small part of the universe which man and his history constitute, and the possibility of other "worlds" in which divine self-manifestations may appear and be received. Such developments become especially important if one considers that biblical and related expectations envisaged the coming of the Messiah within a cosmic frame. . . . The function of the bearer of the New Being is not only to save individuals and to transform man's historical existence but to renew the universe.'[1] Tillich's position is that for the cosmic dimensions his concept of the New Being in the context of his philosophy of Being is more adequate to cope with whatever possible circumstances there may be in the universe. The term 'Christ' is too bound up with man and his history. New Being is essential by being manifested under the conditions of existence, conquering the gap between essence and existence. For men the manifestation of the New Being is Christ who is therefore the centre of human history. Christ is 'God-for-us'. But God is not only for us, he is for everything created. . . . In faith it is certain that for historical mankind in its unique, continuous development, as experienced here and now, Christ is the centre. But faith cannot judge about

[1] *Systematic Theology*, Vol. II, p. 110.

6

the future destiny of historical mankind and the way it will come to an end.[1] Jesus is the Christ for us, namely, for those who participate in the historical continuum which he determines in its meaning. This existential limitation does not qualitatively limit his significance, but it leaves open other ways of divine self-manifestations before and after our historical continuum.[2] For Tillich, incarnation is unique for the human story, but it is not unique in the sense that other singular incarnations for other possible worlds are excluded. Tillich would deny that man alone occupies the sole possible place for incarnation. Tillich thus rules out the necessity, even if it were within the bounds of possibility, of interstellar evangelisation![3]

In Teilhard, what Tillich calls the New Being, he is content to call the Christ. Teilhard clearly uses the term Christ in a cosmic sense, and of course this corresponds with the New Testament view of the pre-existent Christ, who is the Logos. Barthian theology in its extreme anxiety to remove any differentiation between a 'higher principle' of, say, the Logos and Jesus Christ as the expression in history of the Logos, has developed the idea that the humanity of Jesus is the humanity of God. In Jesus alone we discover

[1] Teilhard had no such inhibitions! The whole of *The Future of Man* was an attempt by faith to see the point, purpose and direction of the present processes of the universe. Teilhard believed that the whole of the created order has an evolving and convergent character. We can no longer be content with saying, merely, that Christ is Lord of Creation, as this formulation satisfied only when the universe was thought of as static. It is not really adequate for a universe in flux, as the movement in creation raises questions about its destiny. Teilhard believed that the centre of both human and cosmic evolution is Christ and the special term he uses for this function of Christ is 'the Omega Point'; see Teilhard's discussion in *The Phenomenon of Man*, pp. 257–264, 268–272, and his 'Note on the Universal Christ' in *Science and Christ*, pp. 14–20, also his essay, 'My Universe', dated 1924 in the same volume, pp. 37–85, pp. 151–173.

[2] *Ibid.*, p. 111.

[3] For an interesting discussion of these and related issues raised by modern knowledge, cf. the articles by Dunstan Jones in *Theology*, lxxi, 577, pp. 291–297; and 578, pp. 342–348.

who man really is in the intention of God. However, this does appear as an attempt to universalise in Jesus Christ that which is Jesus, as well as that which is the Christ. Tillich would have regarded any attempt to universalise Jesus as a distortion. In the context of this argument, great care is needed to distinguish between the cosmic Christ and Jesus who is the Christ, otherwise there is a danger, so it seems to me, that we make incarnation as we know it in Jesus Christ the only possible mode of incarnation. As we have seen, Tillich is concerned expressly to deny this conclusion. To put it another way, in so far as corporeal, intelligent life on other planets may have evolved from combinations of different chemicals from those involved in human evolution, how far could the net result be described as 'humanity'? We may, therefore, gladly accept the suggestion that the humanity of our Lord is God's humanity, and that in our Lord we discover who man is in God's creative intention, provided this suggestion is not taken as a warrant for the universalisation of humanity, but, rather, is seen as the miracle of divine grace and condescension that the New Testament described in John 1:14 and Philippians 2:7f. It appears that McKelway's criticism of Tillich's christology does not allow for this cosmic dimension.

In summary, Bonhoeffer develops a christology which speaks directly to man in his modern world faced with his modern problems. His christology has social, ecclesiastical and political meaning. Tillich presents us with a philosophical christology, facing new and profound questions quite fearlessly, whilst Teilhard presents us with a supremely religious christology, firing our imaginations and devotion with his poetic artistry and the sweep of his vision. The value of Bonhoeffer's work is that it brings christology down to earth; Tillich shows us the unanswered questions and implications of Teilhard's sweep, whilst Teilhard in his own way, provides a corrective to the others: he helps us to climb into Elijah's chariot and see and feel the shekinah glory of christology for ourselves.

EIGHT

Ecclesia Quaerens: the Future of Christian Doctrine

ANTHONY HANSON

In July 1917 Teilhard wrote to a friend: 'There must, then, be organised under the direction of the *Ecclesia docens*, an *Ecclesia quaerens*.'[1] He wanted a seeking Church under the direction of the teaching Church. The two Latin phrases outline between them the problem which exists for Christian doctrine today, and indicate, of course, how very much Teilhard was aware of the problem. It could be called the problem of openness: compared with the traditional theologians a hundred years ago, modern theologians of nearly all traditions are far more open-minded. They are far less certain that they possess absolute truth or the whole of the truth. They are far more ready to listen to what is claimed as truth by non-Christians or heterodox Christians. They have for the most part ceased to be shocked by any alleged expression of Christianity. They are much less dogmatic. The reasons for this are not altogether creditable to the apologists for Christianity during the last hundred years. In fact Christian theologians are being compelled to accept a certain intellectual humility today largely because so many of their dogmatic pronouncements in the past have proved wrong

---

[1] Quoted in *The Religion of Teilhard de Chardin* by H. de Lubac (E.T., London, 1967), p. 248.

and have had to be abandoned. But, for whatever cause, this modern openness is to be welcomed. It has enabled Christianity to survive in the West as a respectable intellectual position. And one of those most plainly responsible for this change of attitude in the Roman Catholic Church at least is surely Teilhard himself. His work is full of warnings that the theologians of his own tradition were ignoring huge areas of new knowledge which they ought to be considering. He was always trying to persuade theologians to adapt an exploratory attitude in areas not yet dogmatically defined. He was himself a brilliant pioneer of this *Ecclesia quaerens* which he demanded.

But there is a *problem* of openness: one can be so open-minded as to have no convictions at all. One could imagine a situation in which Christian doctrine virtually disappeared altogether owing to the immense variety of interpretations which could be put upon Christianity, a situation like that of modern Hinduism, for instance. Hindus are proud that theirs is a religion without a definite body of doctrine. Instead of that, they have an immensely varied practice, from extreme spirituality to grossest animism, and a series of alternative religious philosophies having nothing very much more in common than a tendency towards monism. Christianity might develop into a similarly varied phenomenon, an immensely heterogeneous praxis, with a series of alternative theologies having nothing much more in common than some sort of reference to Jesus of Nazareth.

Those who view this prospect with dismay (and I imagine that all catholics and most protestants outside the radical camp can be included in this category) will want to find some outline of Christian doctrine, some *regula fidei* which will be recognisably continuous with the faith of the New Testament and of the Christian Church through the ages. They will require, in fact, that this welcome openness should not be without limit, but should be based on certain fundamental Christian convictions. The question is, of course: how to be open yet convinced? How to preserve both an *Ecclesia quaerens* and an *Ecclesia docens*? I believe that this is the major question for church theologians today, and this essay is written in the conviction that Teilhard de Chardin can help us in tackling it.

I

He can help us primarily because he was himself a splendid example of a Christian theologian in the catholic tradition who was both open and committed at the same time. We will examine briefly both these sides of his character, and then seek to extend our examination by comparing him with two other categories of thinkers, modernists and process philosophers. These may seem strangely assorted categories at first, but we hope to show that a comparison with each category brings out some important aspect of Teilhard's work. We shall end by trying to draw some conclusions as to how his example can illuminate our problem.

We need not spend long in demonstrating that Teilhard was open on the side of modern science. His whole life could be described as an attempt (posthumously successful) to persuade his own Church to accept the conclusions of science in the sphere of biology. Much of the opposition he encountered from inside his own Church was caused by his cosmological speculations. Many people think that his main reputation consists in the fact that he was a philosopher of science. But it is not only in his writings that this openness appears: he was in person a representative of Christian openness. He spent long periods in the sole company of fellow scientists, most of them non-Christians, and he won their respect and admiration. If ever there was a man who symbolised the Christian presence among scientists, it was he.

There is also evidence that Teilhard was prepared to be remarkably open towards non-Christian religions. He was not an expert in the comparative study of religions, nor a sinologist in any serious sense. It is surprising that, despite his long residence in China, he apparently never learned any form of Chinese language. But he had an open attitude towards Chinese Buddhism. Consider, for example, this quotation from his *Letters to Léontine Zanta*. He is comparing Confucianism with Buddhism: 'But side by side with this

empircism . . . there existed . . . the old Buddhist pre-
occupation to sound the rhythm of the world, to establish a
perspective of its countless evolutions, to await the supreme
Buddha who is to redeem all things . . . (this) confirmed me
in my hope that we could perhaps learn from the mystics of
the Far East how to make our religion more "Buddhist"
instead of being over-absorbed by ethics (that is to say too
Confucianist), and at least discover a Christ who is not only
a model of good conduct, but the *super-human* being who, for
ever in formation in the heart of the world, possesses a
being capable of bending all, and assimilating all, by vital
domination.'[1]

This goes far to remove the impression we might gain from
some of his other writings that he had a rather occidental
attitude towards the great religions of the East. This is surely
just the sort of openness to other religions that many Christian
theologians are recommending today.

But even more important and significant in Teilhard is his
determination to be open to the future, to use his Christian
insight in order to illuminate new areas of knowledge. This
it is perhaps that distinguishes him from almost all other
theologians who were his contemporaries, with one or two
notable exceptions such as Charles Raven. Owing to the
anti-modernist reaction initiated by Pius X in the Roman
Catholic Church, and the 'neo-orthodoxy' inspired by Karl
Barth in the Reformed tradition, most theologians in
Teilhard's life-time were engaged in looking backwards,
either to patristic and mediaeval tradition, or to biblical
theology. Indeed it could be said that ever since the Auf-
klärung Christian theologians have been engaged in a series
of rearguard actions; or they could be compared to men in a
besieged city under constant assault from an enemy outside.
All they can do is to rush from one position to another,
attempting to repel the attack as it shifts from point to point.
Teilhard de Chardin wanted to take the initiative; he wanted
to bring the light of Christ to bear on the great new areas of

---

[1] *Letters to Léontine Zanta* (E.T., London, 1969), p. 57–8.

the universe that were being discovered. He took the offen-
sive as a theologian, and actually claimed that Christian
insight could illuminate the course of evolution, could even
help us to understand something about the future. His claims
have been rejected by many; he has been accused of applying
biological categories to what are social phenomena. But
Christians at any rate have no right to disparage his inten-
tions. Teilhard himself was always ready to admit that he
might be wrong; but he did expect that those who sought to
prove him wrong should advance alternative explanations
for the phenomena which he claimed to illuminate. Too
often his critics have been content to reject his conclusions
without suggesting how they themselves could set about
answering the questions which he was trying to solve. In his
conviction that Christianity can be an exploratory intellectual
force as well as an apologetic, Teilhard was entirely ad-
mirable.[1]

On the other hand it is equally obvious that Teilhard was
a thoroughly committed Christian: a loyal member of the
Society of Jesus; a priest who had a deep devotion to the
eucharist; a believer who renewed his consecration to Our
Lord daily. No one could possibly doubt his conviction.
More than this, as a theologian he had a positively christocentric approach. Indeed, it could be said that his theology
was anchored in Christ at two points. He lived 'in Christ'
and found Christ in the eucharist and in the experience of
the Church. But he also regarded the universe as converging
on Christ. Thus he knew both a present Christ and a future
Christ. Not of course that the future Christ was a purely ideal
figure. He was identical with the Christ of present experience,
one with the Christ of the incarnation. The comparison with
Karl Barth here is very interesting. Barth is perhaps of all
theologians who have ever lived the most utterly christocentric: but he was centred on the Christ of the New Testament;

[1] See two excellent articles by A. O. Dyson, 'Man in Evolution' in
Theology, lxxii, No. 585 (March 1969), pp. 98–102 and 'Teilhard de
Chardin, Pierre' in *A Dictionary of Christian Theology*, ed. A. R. Richardson
(London, 1969).

not only the 'Jesus of history', but the Christ preached by the apostles, expounded by Paul, profoundly presented by John, experienced by Christians in every generation. Teilhard added to this another dimension, one found, it must be conceded, in some parts of the New Testament, notably Colossians and Ephesians. This is the cosmic Christ, the Christ towards whom humanity is moving. We do not know Teilhard's views on what is usually called christology, that is the study of the person of the incarnate Son; perhaps they would differ little from those of the contemporary theologians of his own Church. But for him christology is not that, it is the study of the cosmic Christ. He has succeeded in projecting his Christian faith into the future, joining it inextricably with his science as well as his philosophy (*hinc illae lacrimae!*). He is thus an outstanding example both of the open Christian thinker and of the committed Christian theologian. This is not only the source of his vulnerability but also of his great strength.

2

We have suggested that we can profitably explore the extent of Teilhard's openness by comparing him with the Modernists. It is necessary, however, to enter a caution here: within the Roman Catholic Church 'Modernist' is still a term of abuse. Strictly speaking, the term only applies to a group of writers and theologians in the Roman Catholic Church at the end of the last century, the most famous of whom were Alfred Loisy, Henri Brémond, George Tyrrell, and Friedrich von Hügel. Widely though they differed in detail, they all had one thing in common, a desire that the Roman Catholic Church should modify its traditional teaching in the light of modern knowledge, and especially in the light of the critical approach to the Bible as elaborated by non-Roman Catholic scholars. I have ventured, therefore, to use the epithet 'modernist' (with a small m) to describe a larger group than that of the Modernists proper. I would use it of Charles Gore, and would use it of Teilhard himself.

This last assertion may seem questionable: Teilhard never

denied any of the dogmas of the Roman Catholic Church, and would certainly have resented being associated with the names of Loisy and Tyrrell. But, if we may define a modernist as one who, standing in the catholic tradition, wants to modify Christian doctrine in the light of modern knowledge, Teilhard was a modernist. Consider this quotation from Teilhard's letters to Léontine Zanta, bearing in mind that these letters express his own opinions unadulterated by any need to avoid offending ecclesiastical authorities. 'What increasingly dominates my interest . . . is the effort to establish within myself, and to diffuse around me a new religion (let's call it an improved Christianity if you like) whose personal God is no longer the great "neolithic" landowner of times gone by but the Soul of the world – as demanded by the cultural and religious stage we have now reached . . . evil (no longer punishment for a fault but "sign and effect" of progress) and matter (no longer a guilty and lower element, but "the stuff of the Spirit") assume a meaning diametrically opposed to the meaning *customarily* viewed as Christian. Christ emerges from the transformation incredibly enlarged. . . . But is this really the Christ of the gospel?'[1] Here, surely, are all the essentials of modernism as I have defined it, including even the uneasy feeling that the effort to accommodate new knowledge may drive one far from the Christ of the Gospels. It is interesting therefore to ask: why did Teilhard not follow the path of Loisy and Tyrrell into a form of religion scarcely recognisable as Christianity? Why was he more like von Hügel, one who sympathised with the aim of the Modernists but remained faithful to the catholic tradition?

It will hardly do to say 'the Modernists had no respect for dogma and tradition, while Teilhard (as we have pointed out) was a deeply committed catholic'. Loisy, for example, continued for some time to claim that his biblical conclusions did not affect any dogma. And Tyrrell at least was a deeply committed Christian; this perhaps was why excommunication seemed to break Tyrrell's heart, while Loisy rather

[1] *Letters to Léontine Zanta*, p. 114.

seemed to flourish on it. One could suggest a number of subsidiary reasons for Teilhard's adherence to Christian tradition. In the first place Teilhard was not a biblical scholar, and therefore did not come so directly and immediately into conflict with traditional attitudes towards inspiration and inerrance as did Loisy. Teilhard's sphere was that of the doctrine of God, man, and nature, not of Christian origins. Conflict came here, certainly, but it was a much more abstruse area, and one in which fewer ecclesiastics would think they were competent. Again, Teilhard soon acquired a definite position in the world of science, and this to some extent protected him, much as Duchesne gained some protection from his position in the sphere of ancient history. There was (in France at least) no such neutral sphere comprising biblical studies in which Loisy could entrench himself. And Loisy, much to his credit, steadily refused to retire into the neutral zone of assyriology in which both Duchesne and many of his ecclesiastical superiors would have been very glad to see him harmlessly ensconced.

Next, we may suggest that circumstances were not quite as difficult in Teilhard's time as during the emergence of Modernism. Pius X, institutor of the stringent campaign against the movement, died in 1914. Throughout Teilhard's life Lagrange managed to keep alive a tradition of conservative critical scholarship, and the suppression of critical study of the Bible was (as we now know) ended by Pius XII in 1943. Teilhard was also capable of being exiled, which could not be done to Loisy owing to his health. Dangerous speculations about the relation of Christ to the cosmos were apparently less dangerous in Pekin than in Paris. Teilhard, like Duchesne, was willing to be silent for the sake of the Church, but unlike Duchesne (and perhaps unlike Henri Breuil), was not willing to keep off dangerous ground. This is indeed one of Teilhard's greatest titles to honour: he was not willing to keep his theology and his palaeontology in separate compartments; he was determined to be both a scientist and a theologian. The pattern of events presented by both Loisy and Tyrrell is of men, beginning with relatively mild attempts

to modify traditional teaching, being met with discourage-
ment, suspicion, and delation to Rome. The opposition takes
the form, not of reasoned argument or sympathetic remon-
strance, but of violent denunciation by those very little
qualified to judge, coupled with demands for recantation or
resignation from central authority without any reasonable
opportunity for defence being given. This treatment pushes
the victims ever farther and farther towards extreme attitudes, and finally brings Loisy to a position of quite unjusti-
fied scepticism about Christian origins and Tyrrell to a vague
immanentism. Teilhard on the other hand receives one sharp
reproof in 1924, followed by exile to China, and after that
no formal condemnation whatever, merely a steady refusal
to let him publish anything theological. This had the effect
indeed of strengthening his resolution not to desert the
territory which the authorities would have liked him to
avoid, and it caused him a great deal of distress and frustration. But he neither abandoned his quest nor defied his
superiors, and emerged, it must be granted, much the greater
saint because of it.

Teilhard always retained a firm hold on the Christian
conception of God, and this really brings us to the centre of
the matter. This it was that carried him through all tempta-
tions, whether of a purely immanental philosophy such as
Bergson's, or of a form of process metaphysic such as we shall
be considering later. Why this was, we do not know; the
simplest and best way of expressing it is to say that his
experience of God in Christ kept him from adopting a
position that would betray his faith. We may suggest, however, that something was due to his purely chronological
relation to Bergson. Both Loisy and Tyrrell were almost exact
contemporaries of the illustrious philosopher (Loisy was two
years his senior and predeceased him by one year); it could
have been very difficult for men in their position not to be
strongly influenced by him. Tyrrell was in fact dazzled by
him: one of his last essays, 'The Divine Fecundity', is a thinly
Christianised religious version of Bergson's thought. Teilhard
on the other hand was twenty-two years Bergson's junior.

He grew up at a time and place where Bergson's influence was very great indeed, and we know that he corresponded with Bergson. But he lived late enough not to be swept away by the famous philosopher's influence. He kept his head philosophically speaking. He was not treated quite as badly by his own Church as were Loisy and Tyrrell. He was perhaps the greatest Christian of the group. We probably cannot hope to say more than that.

The comparison of Teilhard with von Hügel is interesting. Here too we have someone like Teilhard, with a strong mystical bent. Here too we have someone who sympathised with modernism (if not with Modernism), but who remained faithful to traditional Christianity. But there, I think, the comparison ends. Teilhard had none of von Hügel's penchant for German idealism; Teilhard's contacts with England were entirely scientific and not at all theological. Von Hügel had much less at stake as far as his Church authorities were concerned than had Teilhard. One other, largely external, point in common might be suggested: both von Hügel's and Teilhard's work has lasted better than that of either Loisy or Tyrrell.

We turn now to a very different sort of modernist, Charles Gore. He certainly seems at first sight an unexpected figure in a gallery of modernists. When he died he was regarded as the standard bearer of anglo-catholic orthodoxy; and much of his episcopate was spent in attempting to curb what he no doubt regarded as Modernism in the Church of England. But, judged by the definition of modernism which we have adopted in this essay, Charles Gore was a modernist, that is to say he wished to retain the essentials of catholicism in faith and practice, while accepting what was true and relevant in modern thought. The two areas in which he judged that modern thought forced a reassessment of their faith on Christians were the understanding of the Bible (especially the Old Testament) and the doctrine of the incarnation. He also showed evolutionary sympathies in his earlier christology. His acceptance of at least the principle of biblical criticism grieved his tractarian friends, though they did not regard him as having lapsed into formal heresy. His acceptance of a kenotic theory of the incarnation was in its time a bold and imaginative step, dated though his actual formulation of his theory may seem today. It earned him at the time a reputation for modernism, though in the long run it probably gained him the intellectual leadership of Anglicanism. There is one interesting passage in Loisy's autobiography in which he actually refers to Gore as being, in 1902, something of a heretic. Loisy was annoyed because Gore had written that Loisy did not accept the 'authenticity' (i.e. apostolic authorship) of the Fourth Gospel. In fact this was quite true, but at the time Loisy had not committed himself to this opinion in print.[1]

Comparison with Teilhard is more difficult, since Gore inherited a distinctly different form of the catholic tradition. By the time he began writing it had become clear that the Church of England, because of its connection with the state, was incapable of excommunicating any of its members for heresy, much though some of its leaders might desire to do so. Thus there was never any danger that Gore should be pushed to extremes, as Loisy and Tyrrell undoubtedly were. Again, on the matter of biblical criticism at any rate, Gore had the great advantage that there already existed in the Church of England a school of moderate, liberal scholars who had set themselves to prove that adoption of the critical approach did not necessarily involve extremes of scepticism. Neither in France nor in Germany (still less in Italy!) was there room in the catholic camp for such men as Westcott, Lightfoot, and Hort. As we study the life of Loisy, it is interesting to speculate as to what might have happened had von Hügel persuaded him to take a post in England, as he hoped to do at one point. As for Tyrrell, he might have availed himself of this tradition, but did not do so. Perhaps the denominational barriers were too high. Perhaps the convert from Irish evangelical Anglicanism never had a real opportunity to appreciate the genius of the Church of England.

[1] See A. Loisy, *Mémoires*, Vol. II, pp. 104–106 (Paris, 1930+).

But above all we may say of Gore what we said of Teilhard: he never lost his hold upon the Christian conception of God. This meant that it was his theology and not his philosophy that had the last word with him. Indeed in the matter of philosophy Gore was at a considerable advantage compared with either the two most famous Modernists or even Teilhard himself. Gore did not suffer from reaction against a compulsory Thomism, as undoubtedly both Loisy and Tyrrell did. Any compulsory metaphysic is dangerous, though no man can avoid being influenced by the prevailing philosophy of his day if there is one. Gore was of course an idealist, and had no difficulty in integrating his metaphysics with his theology. In this respect also we may find a link with Teilhard: Teilhard managed to cope adequately with the Thomism which as a Jesuit he officially accepted. He was bound to require some sort of a modification of Thomism, since Thomas's system is static and Teilhard's was necessarily dynamic. But Teilhard was apparently able to make this adjustment without incurring trouble from above. After all, even at the height of the anti-modernist campaign, it could have been awkward to condemn publicly an eminent Jesuit solely because he was not an orthodox Thomist.

But there is one more consideration which the contemplation of Charles Gore's career prompts: Gore attained high office in the Church of England; he was consecrated bishop before he was fifty. A really macchiavellian pope would have appointed Alfred Loisy bishop of Châlons and made George Tyrrell Provincial of the Society of Jesus in England. In fact Loisy was apparently quite a serious candidate for the see of Monaco in 1902 only six years before his excommunication. But by that time Leo XIII was a nonagenarian! Admittedly Gore was born with a silver spoon in his mouth: he had only to refrain from showing marked incompetence, and his social position would have brought him some sort of dignity in the Church of England sooner or later. Admittedly Loisy came from a small farming family with no ecclesiastical interest, and Tyrrell was doubly an outsider as both a convert and an Irishman. They had no hope of high preferment in the normal course of events. The point is, however, that high office had on Gore exactly the effect which (we must presume) the Roman Catholic authorities hoped that official suppression would have on Loisy and Tyrrell: it made him less extreme, more responsible. It changed him from being the spearhead of new thinking to becoming the champion of orthodoxy. It was probably the responsibility of office more than anything else that impelled Gore to draw that arbitrary line between criticism of the Old Testament and criticism of the New Testament which we find in his works. A comparison of Teilhard with Gore shows clearly both how much a man's belief is influenced by his office, and how dangerous to an institution an intellectual can be who is connected to it in a relation of irresponsibility. Prospective heretics are best dealt with by inclusion not exclusion. Innocent III was wiser in his generation than either Pius X or Pius XI.

3

A comparison of Teilhard with modernists has brought out an essential feature of his theology as an 'open' catholic thinker. He was faithful to the fundamental Christian conception of God. Now another set of comparisons will be explored, a comparison of Teilhard as philosopher with some of the process philosophers. We have already noted his relation to Bergson: Teilhard could not help being influenced by him, but must have been alerted to his dangers by the unfortunate examples of Loisy and Tyrrell. The comparison I propose to institute in this section is with two English process philosophers, Alexander and Whitehead. There is no evidence, as far as I know that Teilhard ever read the works of either. But this may not be a disadvantage – coincidences and dissimilarities will be all the more significant for not having been planned.

We find a remarkable agreement between Teilhard and both these philosophers at three points, and an equally remarkable dissimilarity at another, all-important, point. The first agreement is in what Teilhard called 'withinness', his contention that human self-consciousness ('reflection', to use his term) is the clearest evidence of a phenomenon which is found at every stage of existence: there is something corresponding to consciousness even among the atoms. This proposition has given perhaps more offence to physicists than any other of Teilhard's theories, but in fact something very like it is found in both Alexander and Whitehead. Alexander writes: 'our universe in its lower levels behaves apparently (does it do so really?) as if endowed with life.'[1] He can say 'The material floor is *assured* of the materiality of the table' (II, p. 104). And here is an even clearer expression of the same thing: 'The values strictly so called . . . are but the highest instance we know of a feature of things which extends over a much wider range, and is founded in the nature of Space-Time itself . . . what evidence there is points in the direction of the universal prevalence of the process' (II, p. 311). This is very like Teilhard's 'withinness' extended throughout existing things. Whitehead's metaphysics was less indebted to evolutionary ideas, and much more closely allied to contemporary physics than was that of either Teilhard or Alexander, so we do not find as clear an expression in his work of anything corresponding to 'withinness', but something similar can be found. Thus: 'Mental activity is one of the modes of feeling belonging to all actual entities in some degree, but only amounting to conscious intellectuality in some actual entities.'[2] Bearing in mind that Whitehead uses 'feeling' in a sense more akin to that given to 'experience' in ordinary language, we may legitimately trace an affinity here. Further quotation on this point would be difficult owing to the intensely technical nature of Whitehead's vocabulary. But it is fair to say that his extremely 'inter-penetrative' view of reality seems to require some sort of 'withinness'.

The second part of affinity lies in the proof for the existence of God. This is not to suggest that any of these three thinkers ever sets out formally to prove God's existence. Ever since Kant's day such an exercise has been out of fashion outside

[1] S. Alexander, *Space, Time, and Deity*, 2 vols. (London, 1927), I, p. 229.
[2] A. Whitehead, *Process and Reality* (Cambridge, 1929), p. 77.

Thomist circles. But in fact all three thinkers arrive at the necessity for God in their systems by very much the same method. Teilhard, as we know, postulates God as 'Omega point'. Evolution, he says, has been moving in a certain direction. It has not ceased to move. If it is to continue as it has done, it must move towards the increase of 'complexity-consciousness', and this process must have a goal. It must have a goal both because a unitary goal is essentially required by the unifying nature of the process; and because in fact it will not work through human consciousness without a goal. This goal is God-in-Christ. It is important to notice that Teilhard is not merely positing God as the ideal necessary in order to keep men striving, though God is this in Teilhard's system. God is also the force which makes evolution work and (in some sense) the form which evolution will ultimately arrive at. Teilhard was well aware that this brought him perilously close to pantheism; but we must accept his assurance that he was not a pantheist. Theologically certainly he was not, though how far his theology was ultimately compatible with his metaphysic may be open to question.

Alexander's God is a tenuous and ambiguous conception. His great two-volume work has Deity on the title page, but we may surmise that, like the imprimatur on the margin of the work of some border-line theologian, it is there more to give his work a certain respectability in the eyes of his readers than because the author had any great interest in the subject. In effect Deity only makes a brief and fleeting appearance at the very end, like the producer appearing to take his bow just before the curtain falls for the last time. One is left wondering whether in fact Alexander's God had yet succeeded in coming into existence by the time the Gifford lectures were delivered. But such as it is, the road towards it is essentially the same as Teilhard's. The proof seems something like this: the existence in men of religious consciousness indicates a need: the need is met by the next stage towards which Space-Time is developing. That stage may be called Deity: 'there is a nisus in Space-Time which, as it has borne its creatures forward through matter and life to mind, will bear them forward to some higher level of existence' (II, p. 346). The nisus can hardly be identified with God, but it may produce God.

God has a much more robust and central part to play in Whitehead's system. God is required as that which perceives (or experiences) every universal and thus guarantees its actuality. He is also, as in Teilhard, that which gives purpose in the universe. 'What is inexorable in God is valuation as an aim towards "order" . . . In this sense God is the principle of concretion.' (p. 345). And 'God is primordially one, namely he is the primordial unity of relevance of the many potential forms' (p. 494). There is even something in Whitehead very like Omega point: 'Creation achieves the reconciliation of permanence and flux when it has reached its final term which is everlastingness – the Apotheosis of the World' (p. 493). Teilhard would never have used such a phrase as 'the apotheosis of the world', but the parallel is remarkably close. Whitehead's God, however, is by no means transcendent. He is the principle of creativity by creating: e.g. 'God is not to be treated as an exception to all metaphysical principles, invoked to save their collapse. He is their chief exemplification. Viewed as primordial, he is the unlimited conceptual realisation of the absolute wealth of potentiality' (p. 486).

The third point of affinity lies in the account of evil and error. Alexander and Whitehead are remarkably in accord here. Both maintain that evil and error are essential to progress, and therefore give them a specific place in their respective systems. Alexander quotes Plato: 'Evil, O Glaucon . . . will not vanish from the earth', and he comments: 'How should it if it is the name of the imperfection through whose defeat the perfect types acquire their value?' (II, p. 420). And Whitehead writes: 'In fact error is the mark of the higher organisms, and is the schoolmaster by whose agency there is upward evolution' (pp. 236–7); and again 'thus the struggle with evil is a process of building up a mode of utilisation by the provision of intermediate elements introducing a complex structure of harmony' (p. 482). There can be no doubt that this is essentially the way Teilhard viewed evil and error, but as a Christian theologian he was naturally more acutely aware of the positive side of evil, and he did strive to do full justice to the suffering and frustration summed up in, and symbolised by, the Cross. He rather complicated matters by a tendency to regard individuation as such as a mark of incompleteness, if not of evil. Thus 'We carry within us . . . the dull, gnawing *pain of the individuation* by which the separation of beings is maintained and plurality persists'.[1] And here is a quotation distinctly reminiscent of the two English process philosophers: 'that same suffering that kills and decomposes is necessary to the being in order that it may live and become spirit. . . . The mechanism of creation demands it'.[2] But this was no dismissal of evil as something that can be relegated to a minor position in the scheme of things: 'The more Man becomes man, the more deeply engrained – in his flesh, in his nerves, in his mind – and the more serious becomes the problem of Evil: evil that has to be understood and evil that has to be suffered.'[3] And he claims for himself a 'realisation of the utter vanity of human effort unless there is both a natural and a supernatural *emergence* of the universe towards some immortal consciousness'.[4] He wrote elsewhere 'it is possible for suffering to be Christified'.[5]

Teilhard's attitude to evil is one of the points on which he was severely criticised, not least by members of his own communion. The comparison with Alexander and Whitehead shows, I think, that his attitude in this matter was a necessary implicate of his philosophical position. Unless one is prepared to go all the way with Kierkegaard and Barth, one can hardly criticise a Christian thinker merely because he works evil into his scheme of things and is not willing to leave it as an

---

[1] From an article called 'Multitude'.
[2] From a private letter.
[3] From a preface by Teilhard to a work written by his cousin.
[4] From a private letter written in 1934.
[5] From a private letter. This and the previous four quotations are taken from H. de Lubac's work referred to above.

irrational surd. I suspect myself that Teilhard's optimism was as much the product of his Christian faith as of his study of evolution. The fact that we live in an age of pessimism on the whole probably inclines us to dismiss Teilhard's optimism as a 'liberal' element. But we must not forget that the New Testament is, by and large, on the side of optimism.

We said above that, as well as three points of affinity, there was also one important point in which Teilhard differed from the process philosophers. It should be quite obvious by now what that point is, Teilhard's doctrine of God. Despite the fact that his proof of God's existence is very like that of Alexander and Whitehead, the God whom he knows and worships is quite unlike theirs. This is because he took his conception of God from the Christian tradition, from the witness of the Scriptures and the experience of the Church, confirmed in his own experience. It is quite unnecessary to elaborate the contrast with Alexander here: the difference between Teilhard's apprehension of God and the poor little ghost who fills the place of Deity in Alexander is immense. It is true, no doubt, that Whitehead had a God much more like the God of the Christians. On p. 485 of *Process and Reality* he does refer to a theology of love, but makes no attempt to work it into his system. It is also true that Christian philosophers today have found it quite possible to accommodate Christian theology to a system of process philosophy, witness the work of Hartshorne and Pittenger. But this is not exactly what Teilhard attempted. Teilhard was not so much an example of *fides quaerens intellectum* as of *scientia quaerens fidem*. The faith which his science found was the Christian faith, ready made, not elaborated out of evolution or any other natural process. If this meant incompatibilities and inconsistencies in Teilhard's system, we are not to be surprised. From one point of view the problem for Christian philosophers today is, how to accommodate the Christian apprehension of a transcendent God into a universe which, if we are to accept the findings of physics only, seems to be a completely self-integrated, autonomous, dynamic process. As a Christian theologian, I would judge that it is to Teilhard's credit that he maintained intact his Christian apprehension of God, and that the sort of God arrived at by the reasonings of process philosophy unaided by revelation is a totally inadequate one.

If we are to describe Teilhard as a philosopher at all, we must surely describe him as a process philosopher. He has too many links with other admitted process philosophers to be able to escape this category. But the same conclusion about him seems to emerge from our study of his philosophy as from our study of his theology: he never lost hold of the basic Christian apprehension of God in Christ. One could, if one was inclined, draw all sorts of interesting corollaries from this: Christian faith cannot do without a metaphysic, least of all in a period when natural science is running out into metaphysics despite all that the Logical Analysts can do to dissuade it. But the Christian philosopher was rightly described by Anselm as *fides quaerens intellectum*, and his first duty is to keep that faith intact; to see to it that the deliverances of science or of autonomous reason do not end by denying Christian experience. His faith in God, and therefore in the universe, convinces him of course that faith and reason cannot ultimately conflict. I would regard Teilhard de Chardin's work as a noble effort to vindicate this faith.

*   *   *   *

We have been looking at Teilhard in three aspects, which we might call prophet, theologian, and philosopher. Before deciding which of these apply best, we should briefly dismiss two others which have been used of him, poet and scientist. The category 'poet' we need not take seriously; those who use it of him usually do so in order to disparage him. At any rate he would not have claimed that in either *The Phenomenon of Man* or *The Divine Milieu* he was trying to write poetry. If he was only a poet, he is not worth our attention. 'Scientist' has a more serious claim for consideration. But it involves us in serious difficulties. In one sense he was an eminent scientist, a distinguished palaeontologist in his own right. But those who claim he is a scientist usually mean more than this; they mean that his speculations about the course and future of evolution must be taken as a contribution to science, to biology perhaps. The great majority of scientists who have considered this claim resent and deny it. We cannot therefore regard the category as entirely appropriate for the Teilhard of *The Phenomenon of Man*. But this does not mean that we may not have some important and interesting things to say to scientists, questions to ask, suggestions to make. In order to be a stimulus to scientific thinking, one does not have to be a scientist. There is a fair parallel here with Freud: he evidently believed that his theories about the Oedipus Complex, the 'religious neurosis', etc., were scientifically proved. Later psychologists have never accepted this claim, but this does not mean that Freud has not been of great value as a stimulus to scientific thinking in the field of psychology.

This leaves us with our original three categories: let us, for the sake of convenience, take 'philosopher' first. Was Teilhard a philosopher? Not in the strict sense: he would not have been offered a chair of philosophy in any university outside America. He did not pay attention to the technical side of philosophy, e.g. he has nothing to say about epistemology. We have already said that if he was a philosopher he was a process philosopher, and (we may add) not a very outstanding one. He could, however, claim a place under the head of philosophy of religion, in the sense that his whole life work was aimed at providing an up-to-date natural theology for Christians. So, if philosophers of religion are genuine philosophers, Teilhard was one undoubtedly.

I would prefer to call him a theologian. This is because, in my view, his doctrine of God is of more importance in his system than anything else, and it was this, as we have seen, that enabled him to withstand the *Zeitgeist*, while others who, like him, ventured in thought beyond the pale of contemporary Roman Catholic dogma succumbed so quickly. His doctrine of the cosmic Christ entitles him to our respect anyway, for few theologians in the past have ventured into this mysterious realm, and he deserves the credit due to a pioneer. I personally believe that the way in which he relates God to matter is more satisfactory metaphysically than the way, for example, Tillich does. Teilhard's account of this in *The Divine Milieu* seems to me a more adequate solution of the problem than Tillich's doctrine of God as 'the ground of being'. There are other aspects of Teilhard's theology less satisfactory than these (e.g. his account of evil), but for these at least he deserves to be ranked as a theologian well worth our study.

But, in the last analysis, it is in the category of prophet in which I suggest Teilhard shines most brightly. It is as prophet that he points towards the solution of the problem with which we began this essay, the problem of how to reconcile *Ecclesia quaerens* with *Ecclesia docens*, how to set Christian theologians on a course which allows for both openness and fundamental Christian belief. Teilhard de Chardin stood for a christocentric theology, rooted in catholic practice, and this, I think, is what we need if Christian doctrine is not to disappear in a cloud of heterogeneous speculation. Both these phrases, 'christocentric theology' and 'catholic practice', need careful explanation. By the first I mean the conviction that God's character was revealed and activated towards us in Christ, from his birth to his resurrection. And by 'catholic practice' I mean something much wider than Roman Catholic or Anglo-Catholic. I believe there is a tradition of reformed catholicism discovered at the Reformation and never entirely lost by either Anglicans, Lutherans, or Reformed. It is being rediscovered by the Church of Rome today. It is illustrated in the one united church in which the catholic tradition has a part. As long as we hold on to this faith and this practice, as Teilhard did, we shall feel completely free to explore the wide areas of knowledge and belief with which the world confronts us today. We shall be perfectly ready to find Christ at work in other religions, as Teilhard was prepared to do. We shall be eager to examine the metaphysical and theological implications of new deliverances in science, whether in physics, biology, or any other branch, a work which Teilhard so brilliantly attempted.

Above all, we shall look forward to the future with optimism, as Teilhard did, confident that our Christian faith is not a fortress to defend, but a light to illuminate whatever human history may have in store for us.

Notes on Contributors

Dr F. A. Turk is a lecturer in the Department of Extra-mural Studies in the University of Exeter. He has specialised in questions concerning evolution and its relation to philosophy.

The Reverend A. O. Dyson is Principal of Ripon Hall, Oxford, and a member of the editorial board of the *Teilhard Review*.

The Reverend R. B. Smith has completed a year of postgraduate work in Exeter University and has now returned to a parish in Canada.

The Reverend Canon Harold Blair, B.D., is Chancellor of Truro Cathedral.

The Reverend W. J. P. Boyd is Rector of Mevagissey in Cornwall and Ecumenical Secretary and Adult Education Chaplain to the Diocese of Truro.

The Reverend Canon Anthony Hanson, D.D., is Professor of Theology in the University of Hull.

Index of Subjects

181

Index of Names